The New Theogony

The New Theogony

Mythology for the Real World

Maria M. Colavito

State University of New York Press

Published by
State University of New York Press, Albany

For information, address State University of New York
Press, State University Plaza, Albany, N.Y., 12246

Production by Dana Foote
Marketing by Lynne A. Lekakis

Library of Congress Cataloging in Publication Data

Colavito, Maria Maddalena.
    The new theogony : mythology for the real world / Maria M.
Colavito.
        p.   cm.
    Includes bibliographical references (p.) and index.
    ISBN 0–7914–1067–6 (CH : acid-free). — ISBN 0–7914–1068–4 (PB :
acid-free)
    1. Myth.   I. Title.
BL304.C63   1992
291.1'3—dc20   91-22107
                                                                                    CIP

10 9 8 7 6 5 4 3 2 1

For Professor Antonio T. de Nicolás, my *Mentor*

Contents ❧

Contents

Mankind today, stripped of myth, stands famished among all his pasts and must dig frantically for roots. . . . What does our great historical hunger signify, our clutching about us of countless other cultures, our consuming desire for knowledge, if not the loss of myth, of a mythic home, the mythic womb? . . . And who would care to offer further nourishment to a culture which, no matter how much it consumes, remains insatiable and which converts the strongest and most wholesome food into "history" and "criticism"?

—Nietzsche[1]

Introduction 🌱

I always begin my mythology course with the following joke:

> One day, Santa Claus, a farmer, and an honest politician were playing poker. At the height of the game, the lights went out. When the lights came back on, the money on the table was missing. Who stole the money?

The answer, of course, is the farmer, because there is no such thing as Santa or an honest politician. Then I tell them another joke:

> One day, the Easter Bunny, an electrician, and a rich college student were shooting dice. At the height of the game, the lights went out. When th lights came back on, the money on the table was missing. Who stole the money?

The students immediately identify the electrician as the culprit. How are they able to make this connection? What information had to be processed in order for them to "get" the

1

joke? What does the essence of the joke have to do with Santa, the Easter Bunny, an honest politician, a rich college student, a farmer, or an electrician? Are these two jokes the same or different? If they are the same, how are they the same? If they are different, where is the original joke? What is the original version? Who wrote it? Why are the last three questions completely irrelevant?

I perform this exercise because I am convinced that the transmission of jokes is the last vestige of popular culture's myth-making technology. To put it simply, the structure of joke telling is essentially the same as that of myth making.

The obvious affinity between these activities is that both are primarily structures for oral transmission and, because of this, require certain mnemonic skills on the part of the "teller" and certain analytical skills on the part of the "hearer." The teller must reconstruct certain key elements in the transmission of a joke, such that the message becomes evident to the hearer. From the hearer's perspective, that message is not directly deduced from the objects or information supplied in the joke per se; rather, it becomes revealed through the exercise of synthesizing these elements to derive meaning. Names, places, and things in a joke are relevant only insofar as they mark certain actions performed by, or attributes common to, that name, place, or thing. Thus, the essential "message" of a joke is not contingent upon the accumulation of nominal data for the purpose of acquiring information or describing a phenomenon, nor is its purpose to elucidate a scenario based on a real or fictitious set of circumstances; rather, its intention lies in a larger, more comprehensive sphere wherein concepts are replaced by images, and the apprehension of these images creates meaning through every re-creation of the story. In this manner, the key to unraveling a joke usually involves some third element: the imaginative capacities of both the hearer and the teller.

Myth operates in essentially the same way. Like jokes, much of the nominal data in myth is more or less irrelevant;

what counts is what the characters *do*. In fact, one of the first things one notices when learning the myths is how limited the acts of the players are, compared with the voluminous list of names of players. Typically, students are asked to memorize these long lists of names; unfortunately, this is the least useful information to learn. Like our jokes, in order to understand myth, one must merely be able to place the characters into an overall paradigm, and then see what they do in the story line. For example, in the preceding jokes, Santa Claus and the Easter Bunny share the paradigm of fictitious holiday figures. By replacing one for the other in the joke, nothing is lost in the meaning of the joke.

Following this analogy for a moment, consider the mythic motif of the dragon/monster slain by the mythic hero. The list of names of the dragon/monster might read: *Python, Typhon, Vtra, Typhoeus, Tiamat, Echidna, Medusa, Chimera, Sphinx.* The name of the hero might be *Zeus, Apollo, Indra, Heracles, Perseus, Theseus, Oedipus,* or *Bellerophon.* The settings of these myths differ, yet the essential act is the same: the "punch line" is that heroes slay dragons/monsters, cross-culturally.

Analyses of the similarities of mythic motifs is always being performed in myth scholarship; two of the most famous on this subject are found in Lord Raglan's *The Hero* and, more recently, Joseph Fonternrose's *Python.* The problem with this type of analysis, however, is that it fails to answer the question "Why?" Why do heroes always slay dragons/monsters? Why are there only a few basic mythic motifs? And finally, why, in myth, is the act more important than the actor? These are the questions that this text shall address in an effort to allow the student of myth an opportunity to experience the overall worldview of the mythopoetic mind.

Definition and Theories of Myth

Many of our misconceptions about myth stem from the modern English connotations of the word. A typical dictionary definition might read, "A story of unknown origin that explains certain beliefs, natural phenomena, or rituals"; or it might simply say, "A story that has little or no basis in fact." Insofar as these definitions apply to certain uses of the word *myth,* they are accepted as legitimate; however, for purposes of this book, which serves to uncover a cohesive cross-cultural understanding of myth and its purpose, they are insufficient. For this reason, we shall turn to the original meaning of the word *myth* in an attempt to alleviate at least some of these linguistic biases.

The word *myth* comes from the Greek word meaning "that which is spoken." In the plural, it means "*the telling* of a story." The importance of this word origin is sometimes forgotten, since the traces of myth come to us, for the most part, through literary sources. Because of this, one might be inclined to "read" them using the same technology that one might use to read the newspaper, for example. This exercise of reading the myths in this manner would be analogous to memorizing all the particulars of a joke but forgetting the punch line.

Because of this issue of orality as it relates to the discernment of myth, many interpretations have passed in and out of fashion, dressing the stories with the fine accoutrements of their particular points of view with little regard for the internal integrity of the entire worldview from which these myths are derived.

Perhaps the first one to be guilty of such an act is Euhemerus (fl. 300 B.C.), who rationalized myths about the gods as distorted history. At the other extreme are those who see certain elements in the myths not as historical or quasi-historical, but as symbolic metaphors for universal truths. The most notable expounders of this approach are Freud and Jung. The problem with these allegorical theories is that often the symbolic metaphors appropriated from the myths are native to neither the myth itself nor the culture in which it was created. Further, there seems to be no universal agreement as to

4

how and through what criteria these "metaphors" operate and ultimately, why they operate in the first place. Finally, all too often the metaphors lose their integrity, because they become the hybrid monsters of modern culture, being used as place markers to substantiate modern psychological, political, or sociological propaganda. An obvious example of this is Freud's use of the term *Oedipus complex*.

The ritual school, which sees myth as linked to ancient ritual drama, is interesting but fails the test of universality. Further, proponents of this theory can never answer the question, "What came first, the ritual or the myth?"

The etiological school of myth says that myths were used to explain natural phenomena. Following this reasoning, modern scientific hypotheses, which also operate in this manner, might therefore also be classified as myth. The truth is, these etiological myths are not myths at all but cognitive theories that operate under entirely different mental faculties from those of myth, though they, too, happen to have been transmitted orally. Recipes are often orally transmitted, as are directions to my house from the neighboring town, but few of us would consider changing certain elements, altering names and focusing simply on the acts, when transmitting these.

What distinguishes a myth from these other orally transmitted statements is the emphasis on the repetition of certain acts that need to be performed in order that the culture remain dynamic. Using these acts performed as a structure, key patterns can be uncovered in these myth narratives that form a cohesive rendering of a mythic view of the cosmos.

Mythology in Four Moves: The Methodology of the New Theogony

"One, two, three, but where . . . is the fourth . . . ?" Plato begins his stunning dialogue about creation (the *Timaeus*)

5

with this curious pun, for it was well known in his time that no creation could ever come about without the inclusion of the fourth, the material realm. Thus, a study of myth, any methodological approach to myth, could never be complete or valid unless it were itself an embodiment of all the elements that interact and together form the structure of the mytho-poetic mind, be it ancient or modern.

In general, we may say that what we call "myth" is a four-fold cluster of actions and mental properties that individually or together account for the necessary and sufficient condi-tions of the mythopoetic worldview, of the nature and work-ings of the cosmos, and of the individuals and groups of individuals within this cosmos.

In short, and for the sake of clarity, these four fundamen-tal acts defining myth are maia, mythos, mimesis, and logos. Each act is a single focus or mental habit; together the four account for the totality of human and divine acts, or mental habits, that have guided the human species to the present shores. Though strictly speaking, myth is merely one of the acts in myth making, even this act is incomprehensible unless the other three mental operations are included in the narra-tives of myth. These four mental habits have acted together or against each other, and at times some have even been sup-pressed altogether, throughout human history; and unless the study of myth encompasses all four aspects of this struggle, we could never retrace the path to the origins of a mythopoetic mind-set, or ever be able to truly interpret myth for human liberation.

Maia (Gr. midwife) is the term used to signify the bring-ing forth of action from inaction, cosmos out of chaos, the initial spark that kindles the mind to transform from nothing to something. It is the midwife between the divine realm of immortality and potentiality and the human realm of tempo-rality and material existence. The aspect of maia in the human sphere is represented by the human faculty of imagining. It is the expression of the creative experience; it cannot be described, it has no form, its proper abode lies in the midregion between the human and the immortal realms. Once an individual begins to interpret or reflect upon the experience, maia disappears and the experience receives an existence of its own, outside the realm of potentiality, and it is given a form, name, boundary. In short, the reflective act heralds in the aspect of mythos. And with mythos the world moves from chaos to cosmos.

Mythos (Gr. delivered by word of mouth) primarily describes the initial reflection of the creative experience. It is the oral transmission of an experience. The aspect of mythos is the first public act, the first act in mythic cosmos, the first "scream of individuation," to quote Nietzsche. Consequently, however, mythos also represents the original fall from grace, the first act that breaks from the unity of the beginning, from the glory of immortality; for the telling of an experience now has another element, an experiencer, a self, through whom the experience flowed. Thus it follows naturally that the telling of the experience is not the experience; it is much less than the experience, and only those who have had the same experience may truly *understand* the full import of the teller's tale. In the mythic aspect, gods and goddesses, monsters, and fabulous geographic realms are created to represent the ideal acts and to create the first boundaries of the human imagination, so that communities of experiencers can share common revelations.

Mimesis (Gr. to make a copy) is the aspect that describes the mythopoetic action of re-membering or re-creating. It is the aspect that retells an experience that has already passed through the reflective process. In this manner, the story is told with an intent, a moral. The elements are carefully selected in a didactic frame. What becomes important now is the story not so much as it relates to the original creative experience of individuals, but as it relates to the desire to make a point. If maia is the experience and mythos is the oral transmission of the experience, then it can be said that the mimetic phase is recognized by the first frozen form: the pictographic mode. Its boundaries are well defined, and the creative experience of the individual all but falls to the wayside in favor of the moral proscriptions and prescriptions superimposed on the telling of the story, which now becomes geared toward establishing the social mores of the collective group.

Finally, *logos* (Gr. the word by which the inward thought is expressed), taking as its *origins* these mores, completely eradicates the level of personal experience and uses the rules derived from the mimetic to create theories about human action. The mores are founded on human experience, but only on hypothetically universal experience—in other words, experience filtered through the sieve of a collective interpretation. As such, then, no origin in logos has the certainty of an origin in maia. By analogy to the act of mimesis, logos ceases to be a pictographic representation; it transforms into a symbolic or alphabetic system that has only its own correlatives within its own framework, with no derivatory capacity from the experiential realm of the individual. Simply put, to know something from logos is very different from knowing something in maia. In the former case, knowledge is acquired by the appropriation of as much data as is possible; the more the better, for the validity of the theory rests upon its measure as compared to the behaviors of the nameless general group. Maia knowledge, conversely, is a certain, exact knowledge that cannot be waived by any outside information, regardless of the general group. Maia knowledge was considered a gift from the gods, humans having been granted this capacity for "insight," while logos had always been the shadow of maia, in the mythopoetic world.

This fourfold division is neither a convenient device for classification, nor an arbitrary tool for interpretation; it is the fabric itself of myth, and as such, it is an abstraction that, though distinguishable, is inseparable from myth. From a biological perspective this fourfold division is the neurophysiological equipment of the species, its mental habits accumulated through the repetition of the past: imagining, fantasizing, narrating, following the discursive path of logic; also making images from nothing, making images from forms already existing, making stories, conceptual thinking and hypothesizing.

From an interpretative stance, *maia* stands for an original experience, while *mythos, mimesis,* and *logos* stand for different ways of making this experience public, either through narrative (mythos), through visual forms (mimesis), or through theory or alphabetic substitutions or conceptual analyses (logos). From a religious viewpoint, maia is the original experience, and the rest is an effort at making it present. Thus in the Eleusinian mysteries, for example, the "mystery" was the fact that, while one could talk about the dramatic reenactment (*dromena/mimesis*), the revelation of sacred objects (*deiknymena/logos*), and the uttering of certain words (*legomena/mythos*), the true mystery could never be uttered, because it lies outside the realm of form, even linguistic form. Maia is that mystery.

Finally, and most importantly from an epistemological point of view, these four acts reflect the overall structure of the oral/aural model, which has as its verification the ancient science of acoustics.[2] In other words, this fourfold system of acts corresponds exactly to the scientific operations functioning within the oral/aural worldview;[3] thus, by analyzing the myths through the criteria of sound as the primary organizer of sensation, the full import of their meaning becomes clear.

The first chapter is an introduction to this oral/aural worldview, what I have termed the model of the "One." This chapter elucidates the differences between our modern foundations and beliefs about the world, labeled the "Zero" model, which rely heavily on the logos act; and the foundations and beliefs that oral/aural cultures espouse, specifically, on the role of maia as the universal source (the One). It also outlines how this shift took place, historically.

Throughout the rest of this book, the four acts of maia, mythos, mimesis, and logos are presented as the structural framework of myth—not only of the major paradigms, but also of the specific attributes of particular deities of any myth system. This is the subject of chapters 2 and 3. In Western mythology, particularly in Greek mythology,[4] this fourfold division of acts is replicated through the paradigms of creation myths (maia); theogonies, including the Sacred Marriage (mythos); hero myths and myths of hubris (mimesis); and myths of transformation and eschatological myths (logos). Similarly, within the Greek pantheon, the gods and goddesses are divided, by the acts they represent, into gods of logos (Athena, Hephaestus, Prometheus, Hades); gods of mythos (Hera, Hebe, Ares, Eileithyia); gods of mimesis (Demeter, Dionysos, Heracles) and gods of maia (Poseidon, Hermes, Aphrodite). Hestia, Zeus, Apollo, and Artemis share a unique position in this scheme. Hestia is the cosmic model of maia; Zeus, the cosmic model of mythos; Apollo, the cosmic model of mimesis; and Artemis, the cosmic model of logos.

In a similar fashion, human acts, copying the models of the gods, replicate the fourfold path in the life choices that individuals make. Chapter 4 outlines these human paths as the material, human, heroic, and mystic. Thus, the path of materialism focuses mostly on the act of logos; humanism, on the act of mythos; heroism, on the act of mimesis; and mysticism, on the act of maia. The collective trend of human choices determines the mythic age that prevails, and naturally, the gods that are worshiped above all others. Thus, a Golden Age would be marked by the act of maia; a Silver Age would have the act of mimesis prevail; a Bronze Age would consider mythic acts to be of most importance; and finally, in an Age of Iron, logos certainly prevails.

The final chapter of this book is really a beginning. This chapter introduces the notion that in the Platonic and Pythagorean philosophical schools this fourfold division of acts not only was operative, but in fact formed the crux of their entire philosophical stances. The famous allegory of the cave and Plato's divided line are reinterpreted to illustrate that

Plato himself utilized this mythic paradigm of the fourfold acts to present his philosophical position. In fact, his divided line, structurally, is also evident in both the *Symposium* and the *Sophist,* where it was used to outline Diotima's speech about love and Plato's discourse on the productive arts, respectively.

The Pythagorean training, interestingly enough, also outlines the fourfold acts of maia, mythos, mimesis, and logos. In fact, not only did the Pythagoreans find the number four useful; it was sacred to them, because they recognized within it the power of all of creation.

Both of these philosophers, well aware of the imminent possibility of a worldview shift away from aurality toward literacy[5] (which naturally would have emphasized acts of logos over those of maia, mythos, and mimesis), strove to maintain, in their schools, training that included all of the habits of the gods. In this manner, they sought to preserve in the human species the capacity of the individual to apprehend the divine, through the exercise of creation by maia. Similarly, the goal of this book is to once again revive all of the acts of the gods to ready the human spirit for the return of the Golden Age.

Chapter I

The Mythic Model: On the One and the Zero

"All things arise from One."

—Anonymous

Suppose for a moment that the preceding statement were true, that Zero didn't exist and that the starting point of all things were One. How, then, would you arrive at the number Two? (If you say by simply adding two Ones together, you are forgetting that there is only one One; therefore, the operation that you are suggesting is not possible in this scheme. Try again.) Sooner or later you would realize that the only way for One to become Two is by division, that is, by One splitting itself in half. What are the ramifications of this act? If One divides itself into Two, then where is the One? Which of the halves of the One is the original One? Both? Neither? Is there a One any longer, or has that One become just one more . . .

Consider further the nature of Two. Two, thus created (by division), contains within it the potentiality of both the same and the different: the same, in that all of it is composed of the One, though technically it loses its quality of Oneness, totality, and unity, once the other is born. Though the other is a copy exactly like the original One, by its mere existence, it cannot be the same as the original One, so in its own act of separation, One simultaneously creates the different, and the One disappears.

A logical consequence of this procedure would create a numerical system, and through *it,* worlds would be created. The names in these worlds, the descriptions of the things in these worlds, the appropriation of forms in these worlds would all be subject to and the result of this simple act of One becoming Many, yet few of us who'd spend our lives counting, naming, reproducing all these things in all these worlds, would probably ever ask the questions, "What would make One want to be Many?", "How does the Many arise from One?", and finally, "Is there a path back to that original unity of the beginning?"

If a cosmological system were to begin with such a unity as One, of which everything is a refracted part, there would be a natural affinity among all the parts, and each part would thus be seen as an individual piece in the larger scheme of things, though each dismembered piece would contain all of the same essentials as the One, save its unity. Once this necessary link were established between the parts and the whole, then the possibility would exist for transformation, communion, and finally, immersion among the parts, and theoretically, at least, even a return to the whole, the unity.

Imagine the consequences of a world thus created. Everything manifest would of necessity be a copy of that which exists within the One, though the One would be much more than each of the elements thus manifested. Since each part would be a copy, then the One would of necessity be the only original. Thus it follows that the original never manifests; that what is seen would only be merely a copy of the original, because it possesses all the parts *but not the whole* or the unity of the original. This means, then, that true reality would exist only in the realm of the unmanifest, that is, in the One. Conversely, illusion would be that which is *seen* in the world of manifested forms, as seemingly independent, disparate entities.

How, then, could any part of the whole experience its origins while still remaining only a part of the whole? And if it were possible to make this journey into wholeness, what would be left of the part? What would have to be sacrificed to achieve this unity? And what would be gained?

"The mysteries of being," evident in these questions, instigated the lifelong quests and the traveled paths of the great mystics of humanity, from Pythagoras to Buddha, to the Christ; and their searches for the link to that original unity marked for the rest of us a continuous lifeline back to the source from which all of life arises. This book provides the map of their journeys, through the study of myth as the universal epistemological foundation of all human experience and the human faculty of imagination that creates myth. Though each traveler forged his or her own path through the landscapes of the soul to this destination of unity, the human faculty of imagination provided the necessary vehicle for each of them in their individual travels. Through the practice and exercises of imagining, they each verified, albeit via independent paths, that the possibility exists for the part to experience the One; without imagining, however, not even the possibility exists.

The Problem with One

That all things arise from the One was a tenet universally acknowledged among early cultures,[1] though the One was envisioned in many ways. For the Greeks, the One was Chaos, the realm of undifferentiated possibility from which all things are born and to which all things return. Later, that force was personified in the goddess Hestia, whose divine fire provided enlightenment, though her fire itself could not be seen. The ancient Hindus embodied this essential unity as Asat, the realm of nonexistence as the following passage describes:

> Then there was neither existence nor non-
>   existence:
> Neither the world nor the sky that lies
>   beyond it;
> What was covered? And where? And who
>   gave it protection?
> Was there water, deep and unfathomable?
>
> Neither was there death nor immortality,
> Nor any sign of night or day.
> The One breathed without air by self-impulse;
> Other than that was nothing whatsoever.[2]

Later, this unity was envisioned as the goddess Kali, whose three manifestations as creator, preserver, and destroyer are described in the following:

> You are the original of all manifestations; you are
> the birthplace of even us; you know the whole
> world, yet none know you ... you are both subtle
> and gross, manifested and veiled, formless, yet with
> form ... Resuming after dissolution your own

form, dark and formless, you alone remain as One ineffable and inconceivable... though yourself with beginning... you are the beginning of all, creator, protector and destroyer.[3]

To begin with the One seems obvious, yet our culture seems to have obstructed the beautiful simplicity of this worldview. Of course the introduction of Zero into the numerical system appears to be at least part of the problem, since it introduces the possibility of nonexistence as "the absence of" rather than "the fullness of," and this distinction necessarily leads to the converse conclusion that existence, then, is that which can be counted and that nonexistence is that which cannot be counted and, therefore, *does not exist.*[4]

Now suppose that we named One, "God." By the criteria of ancient cultures, that is, those who see One as the origin of things, the name of God, as well as all the attributes of God, would remain the same as if we were to call One "Chaos" or "Asat" or "Hestia" or "Kali." Think for a moment of what would happen to God, though, in a system where Zero is the beginning. God here would not be One; he would merely be one more, if anything at all.

Now imagine that a cosmological system were to be derived from Zero, and not One. How could it possibly be apprehended? Certain precepts would first have to be posited, namely that somewhere, somehow, something *became.* In order to posit this, simultaneously, we must also posit that there was a beginning, namely, a marked moment when something came of nothing. This event then would herald in the conception of historical precedence, namely, of time as we know it. Following this further, since the possibility existed for one thing to randomly occur as arising from nothing into something, the possibility exists for anything to independently occur in this manner. Thus two principles could now be derived from this scheme:

- That each thing is independent unto itself.
- That that which is, is that which manifests.

Imagine now a world based upon these principles. The beginning, middle, and end of things would be determined only by those things themselves. Communal efforts would merely mean the consensus of individual things acting in communion for their common benefit, which, of course, would be the preservation of their individuality. There would be no need of justification for action, nor would there be criteria for action in favor of one manner over another. If things *could* be done, or created, they *would* be. Finally, there would probably be an inexhaustible struggle for stability, immobility, and preservation of things, since all that would constitute existence would be things that are manifest; therefore, the dissolution of the manifested form would constitute its cessation. Then death would mark the end point of the existence of the thing, after which time it would once again become nothing.

The human faculties allow for both of the above interpretations, and therefore embodiments, of the cosmos. Using the faculty of cognition (including systems of logic; inductive, deductive, and transcendental methods, etc.; and the intuitions derived from them), worlds are created by positing the existence of things, in much the same manner as was done when attempting to create a world by beginning with Zero. The imagination, which is only a faculty of creation, works by taking as a given, that the origin of all things is One. No human is free without the capacity to exercise both of these human faculties, yet our faculty of imagination, for whatever reason, has become all but eradicated from the realm of human possibilities, and with it our hope for true freedom. It is time to recall our imaginative capacities, before we are no longer able to do so. It is time to recover myth from the recesses of our dusty souls.

How These Two Models Operate

The simplest description of how these two models operate and are distinguished from one another is discussed by Ernest McClain in the following passage:

> There are two different and contradictory (epistemological) models grounding the meaning of sentences, cultures, and whole philosophies. One model takes sight and its criteria as the primary organizer of sensation. On a model of sight a language of substance is born to communicate exactly what the model had previously established: atomic things and events, within a visual space ruled by fixed coordinates of space and time. On the model of sound . . . a language is born for communication which emphasizes perspectives not of the same fixed object, but of a multitude of relations which must appear for any object seemingly to appear.[5]

McClain here is articulating a distinction discovered by Antonio de Nicolas in his work on the early Hindu texts of the Rg Veda. This distinction between aural and visual epistemological models is the foundation of the varying approaches in our previously discussed models (of creation by the One and creation by Zero).

The model of creation by the One is the aural model.[6] This model produces mythology, geometry, alchemy, polytheism, music, mysticism, and enlightenment through revelation. The model of creation by Zero is the literary model. It is responsible for theology, algebra, biology, monotheism, visual art, asceticism, and knowledge through the appropriation of data. Humanity needs both models. Our modern culture has focused on the skills necessary to produce only the latter model. A simple journey through history reveals that this struggle between these two worldviews is not new.

Historical Glimpses

While our modern emphasis on the literary (Zero) model is a direct result of the scientific revolution brought about in the end of the sixteenth century,[7] prior to that time, traces of this epistemological worldview appeared as lapses in the overall development of many cultures. I should like briefly to discuss some occasions of these lapses in particular: in ancient Egypt, during the Armana period; and in Greece, through the philosophical works of Aristotle.

The Armana period of Egyptian culture was marked by the reign of the heretic king Akhenaten (1372–55). Akhenaten,[8] who was formerly named Amenhotep IV, instituted perhaps the greatest religious revolution in ancient times by declaring the supremacy of the god Aten (solar disc) to the exclusion of all the other gods, especially the deity Amen (the hidden one). Prior to the reign of Akhenaten, Egyptian religion, though diverse in its iconographical expression, tended toward viewing the universe on the model of the One:

> Ancient Egyptian speculation about the origin and nature of the universe ... strongly tended towards explaining the apparent plurality of the cosmos in terms of an underlying unity. One system, ... 'Heliopolitan,' opted for Atum, ... the one; ... the Memphite system exalted 'Heart' as the primal element; ... Hermopolis described the primal element as the infinite ... completely hidden.[9]

Akhenaten's god, however, was not like these deities. Where the others boasted of their god as being the "*One from which* all things come," Akhenaten's Aten was known as the "*unique creator* of all things."[10] While the other deities were given epithets such as the "hidden one," Aten was the "visible one" (the physical sun in the sky). Aten had no myths, no anthropomorphic artistic rendering, few epithets. In fact, Aten was an exclusive deity, as is evidenced by Akhenaten's orders to deface temples of other deities, to all but eliminate temple acts and offerings to other deities, to discard mythology, and to remove the importance of the eschatological literature.

Finally, and most importantly for our discussion, Akhenaten's reign is marked by a change in the hieroglyphic style and artistic style.[11] Words tended to be written phonetically, rather than pictographically, and the artistic rendering of the sun disk was effectively static: the god of the sun did not change his shape, he did not manifest in any other way than the manner in which he appears in the sky; in short, he represented stability, permanence, and unyielding omnipotence. This shift is a major divergence from the cultural norm of ancient Egypt.

And if one thinks that this mind-set of a unique, creator god was eradicated with the destruction of Akhenaten's reign, one ought to read the writings of St. Augustine, who seems to have taken up Akhenaten's view in interpreting his own Christian God:

> What did God make before he made heaven and earth? . . . I say that our God is the Creator of every creature: and if by the name 'heaven and earth' every creature is understood; I boldly say, that before God made heaven and earth, he did not make anything.[12]

God here is clearly depicted through the "Zero model" worldview. As an entity outside of creation, unlike the One, he remains detached and separate from his orphaned creations. There is no link among his creations except for the fact that they were all created by him, albeit independently of each other. In other words, each created being has affinity only to its creator, of which the creation is *not* a part. And God, in this model, is merely the artificer of forms that are created in space/time, and then later in time, he is the destroyer of those forms that he created.

What seems to have contributed to this strange shift from the One model to the Zero model in the field of religious enquiry is the human technological shift from the ear to the eye as the primary organizer of sensation, as the following examples shall show.

Ancient Greek thought from the time of Homer to the time of Plato was grounded on the model of the One, though as in Egyptian culture, there were many varied representations of this belief: Hesiod named it "Chaos," the Ionians applied various elemental appellations to it, Empedocles and Pythagoras simply referred to it as "the One," and Plato *named this force* "God."[13] Implicit in these renderings is the notion that the realm of the One is the source of all things, yet *it*, strictly speaking, has no form.

Knowledge, therefore, was seen as a result of training to re-create and thereby establish the continuity of an *act* similar to that act performed by the One. That is, the means of obtaining knowledge was through the experience of action. The evidence of the relative worth of the experience was apparent in the manifested form.[14] All of this was changed by Aristotle due to two of his philosophical allegations.

The first shift has to do with Aristotle's introduction of and preoccupation with substance, which led him to the fatal conclusion that *being was substance*.[15] Following this, it is not difficult to see how his next query established a necessary link to this one that completed his philosophical quest. That is, that knowledge, then, became equated with explanation about substances. Thus, what Aristotle amputated from philosophical speculation, namely, the experiential source of knowledge through acts of the *doer*, was replaced with a system of categorization and classification of things through the criteria of logic. *Knowledge* then was reduced to *knowing about.*[16]

It must be noted, in all fairness, that Aristotle himself was not rejecting the earlier oral worldview by his philosophical methodology; in fact, he acknowledged the necessity of both. It is the later philosophical thinkers who applied *this method to the exclusion of others,* who are responsible for the present state of affairs. Perhaps the clearest example of such a thinker is René Descartes,[17] whose first *Discourse on Optics* heralds the dawning of the visual (Zero) model, with its emphasis on sight as the primary sense, and his introduction of the mathematical model (with emphasis on measure and order) as the universal determinant of knowledge.

Each of the above examples from history points to the origins of certain elements in the embodiment of the Zero model: the preference for stability and permanence over mobility and change; the emphasis on things that are seen as the source of knowledge and not on the acts performed to create them; and finally, the belief in nonexistence as the source to which all things return. Taken as a whole, these glimpses from history reveal humanity's attempts to superimpose their own wills onto the larger scheme of the cosmos, in an effort to control or perhaps disguise the underlying truth that all things arise from the One, including themselves.

The One Made Myth versus Zero Made Theory

The model of the One takes for granted the necessity of the fourfold acts of maia, mythos, mimesis, and logos; in fact, the earliest myth cycle evident in almost all cultures, that of the triple goddess, outlines how the goddess in her four aspects and three forms fashions the model of all creation. The goddess, through the pattern of the lunar cycle, forms cosmos and then dissolves it back to Chaos, in an everflowing cycle of life, death, and rebirth. In this myth system, what we modern interpreters might term a "creator deity" is made only in the second phase of the cycle and is given a form only in the mimetic third phase of the cycle. And in the fourth phase of her cycle, this deity is sacrificed back to maia, his original mother.

Reinterpreting this cycle from a Zero perspective, namely, from one that focuses on forms, things, objects, and not the power of creation, it is easy to see how this mimetic "creation of forms" phase could be misread or overemphasized to reduce all of creation to the forms created, thereby raising the status of the mimetic creator deity (demiurge) to sole, omnipotent, omniscient (male) deity. This is what occurs when a logos theory of interpretation is superimposed on creation myths. In effect, what occurs is that, as we stated in the Introduction, the mimetic act serves as the origin of logos; therefore, the creative act of maia disappears altogether (since the focus in this phase is on cataloging the mimetic forms in order to derive theories), and what is left is a theory about how some creative demiurge "out there" (separate and distinct from ourselves and his creations) made forms out of nothing! This theory is easily verified, through a total (mis)interpretation of the original mythos, and this serves as the origin of the theory of creation—entirely abstracted from the mimetic phase and totally devoid of individual human experience.

So that the reader may see, at a glance, how these two models operate, I present the original triple-goddess myth cycle to clarify both the role of maia, the mother as creator; and the role of logos, the absent father as the surrogate usurper of the same role. The models of the One and the Zero will then become starkly evident.

Revisioning the Triple Goddess

The mysteries of maia are embodied in the myths of the goddess, manifested in her three forms. As the triple aspects of virgin, mother, crone, she is the universal archetype for the creation, preservation, and dissolution of worlds. She is the metamorphosing lunar sphere; she is the yonic triangle; she is the One in Three, the perfect "form" of transformation, the original Trinity.

Every ancient culture revered the goddess in her triple manifestations. In India, she was Kali-Ma; the Druids called her "Diana triformis"; in ancient Etruria, she was "Uni" (a cognate of *Yoni*); in Egypt she was called "Isis." Every aspect of the divine feminine as creator, preserver, and destroyer of forms was made present to the members of these cultures through the sacred mystery practices, and these practices have been preserved for us through the mythic tradition. The difficulty, of course, is in our lack of expertise in "reading" the myths within this context of maia, as the source of creation.

The Four and the Three

There are four phases of the triple-goddess myth cycle. These phases correspond cosmically to the acts of maia, mythos, mimesis, and logos; naturally, to the phases of the moon; and biologically, to the rhythm of woman. What is of vital importance is that these myths, while appearing to mark a path of degeneration, actually recall a cyclical process of creation, preservation, and dissolution. Therefore, the seemingly destructive phase of logos, in this model, is in actuality a mythic description of the return back to the original unity of the One.

Phase One: Chaos, Golden Age, New Moon, Maia

The new moon is that phase in the lunar cycle where there is no manifested form of the moon visible. This lack of definite form places the empirical moon in the realm of potentiality. Since it does not contain any particular form (which would be subject to dissolution), it is, at this stage in the cycle, in the state of Chaos, of "undifferentiated possibility." Because the gravitational force of the moon, during this phase, is operating in conjunction with that of the sun (as it relates to earth), this phase corresponds to the mythic Golden Age, the cosmic season of eternal spring.

The goddess in this phase is usually described in terms of her powers of action rather than by physical description. Here she is revered as that most sacred, nameless power: maia.

Phase Two: The Virgin, the Androgyne, Mythos

The second phase of the goddess myth corresponds to the lunar cycle with the appearance of the crescent moon, the "horns of Diana," the first manifested form of the moon. In this phase the goddess is the virgin, created by the "breaking open" of the One. Here the gravitational forces of sun and moon begin to struggle against each other in their relationship to the earth; hence, the emergence of the opposites: positive/negative, male/female, darkness/light. As the first "image" of the One, the virgin is the manifested shadow of the perfect one: she is the realm of potentiality *in fluid form,* of mythos. As the moon moves toward its half phase, the virgin and her opposite male "twin" (as in the case of Artemis and Apollo) represent the mythic division of the One and, simultaneously, the dissolution of the original unity, now that manifestation has taken place. Each aspect of the duality screams out its individuation. They are two equal aspects vying against one another for permanence of form. In the cosmic cycle, this aspect represents the mythic time when the world becomes divided into two seasons, winter and summer. For the first time, vegetation must die to be reborn.

Myths recounting the virgin aspect of the triple goddess depict her as the androgynous youth Artemis, who rivals her brother Apollo in skill with the quiver and bow, who roams about in the forests protecting the hunted and hunter alike. Sometimes the virgin is the warrior goddess Athena, born armed with a warrior's garb, whose sole concerns are to offer strategic counsel in warfare and promote logical wisdom among the populace. These goddesses do not concern themselves with issues of creation; they are stagnant vestiges of the awakening of the I. The virgin aspect is the One realizing her own reflection and, being mesmerized by her power to create such a beautiful form, seeking to preserve it at all costs.

Phase Three: Full Moon, Mother/Lover, Mimesis

The sexual union of the opposites yields the "mirror image" of the One; namely, a mimetic re-creation of a manifested form that embodies the qualities of the One, *except that it is manifest* and is thereby subject to decay and dissolution. This is geometrically imagined by the circle of the full moon. The full moon represents the fecundation of the virgin through the infusion of the male, who at the moment of conception loses his own identity and "dies," that is, loses his form. Likewise, in this act the virgin sacrifices her individuation; however, not by killing herself, but merely by removing her shadow and allowing the male to return to her. Thus, for transformational creation to occur, the male must die through dismemberment; the female must re-create him through love. This phase only comes about when the virgin turns away from the mirror of I and sees that all she lacks, to return to the unity of the beginning, is her distance from her twin. The male, to effectuate this phase, recognizes the temporality of his form and realizes that only in his own dismemberment shall there be a hope for his own immortality, and thereby assents to the act. Unless this occurs, the progeny of these two opposites yields more stagnant, forms created as shadows, not of the original One, but merely as shadows of the *forms* of their parents.

This is the mimetic phase where the reunion of the opposites yields a new, creative element of changeable, material form. In this age the children of the cosmic "opposites" begin to war with one another, fighting for possession of the forms. There is also born in this act, however, the heroes: male children born out of the fusion of immortal and mortal (that is, children born from the dismemberment of the male element: the forms made of the reflected light of the sun and the maia power of the female). These are the children who effectuate the transformation of the cycle back to its original unity.

The strongest mythical references to this third phase usually involve the abduction of the triple goddess in her virgin aspect by the god of death, or a dying hero who is brought back to life by his female consort, who is usually depicted as the bride of death or goddess of the underworld. Here all the references to death and dismemberment and then resurrection become evident. The most famous myths of these types are those of Hades and Persephone and Isis and Osiris. In both cases, the male/female dualities are siblings/lovers who restore the continuity of creation through their mimetic acts of dismemberment and re-creation.

The other aspect of this phase occurs after the goddess gives birth to her child, usually a son, who is made in the "image" of her (absent) lover, the sun. Variations on the myths of the goddess in this phase occasionally have her mating with this son/lover. These myths refer to the same act as above, except "the mother" here refers to the goddess as the original *manifested* One; therefore, the male counterpart in the act of creation would be considered her son, not her twin. Since the aspect of the full moon is the exact opposite of the new moon, this inversion to son/mother replaces the duality of opposites of the second phase. In this phase, however, the absent partner is the masculine paternal force, while in the second phase the absent partner is the feminine One. This is the portion of the triple-goddess myth that becomes most troublesome: Does the full moon then symbolize the *hieros gamos* (the return of the two halves back to the unity of the beginning), or does it represent the birth of the child of the cosmic pair (sun and moon); and is it therefore an exaltation of the sun, the son of the sun on earth?

In the maia model, the full moon represents *both* the *hieros gamos* and the birth of the son, for both are necessary components for the goddess cycle to continue. At the full moon phase, the male and the female elements of the opposites are both sacrificed back to the One, maia (thus the "circle" of immortality), in order to re-create—in this case the son. When, however, the epistemological paradigm shifts from the One to the Zero model, the full moon represents *only* the son: the "image" that is similar to but not like his father, the physical form of the sun. Thus the son rules over the sublunar, mortal realm as his father rules over the celestial one.

From this moment on, then, the son begins his journey of sacrifice, which is described in our discussion of the next phase. How this sacrifice is interpreted and to whom he is sacrificed, however, depend upon the model, once again. In the Zero model, which focuses on the form of the son, the son is sacrificed back to his father, the original light. In the One model, the son is sacrificed to his original mother, maia.

Phase Four: Crone, Iron Age, Waning Moon, Logos

This final phase of the triple-goddess myth cycle is perhaps the most misunderstood and has done the most damage to the modern psyche. From exotic images of flesh-eating hags devouring corpses of young (male) children to myths of mothers crying helplessly as their sons are being taken away to die, the iconographic and mythic depictions of this final phase of the lunar/goddess cycle has been popularly dubbed the "doomsday" aspect. As the moon slowly begins its return back to the new phase, one observes that its image begins to deteriorate from the ripe fullness of the glowing orb, to the half moon, to the crescent, and then finally back to formlessness. This seemingly degenerative portion of the lunar cycle is in reality simply a return of the moon back to the position of regeneration, back to the new-moon phase. It is not the ultimate dissolution of the moon herself; rather, it is the dissolution of the old cycle and, simultaneously, the culmination of the new cycle.

Interpreting this cycle from the Zero perspective, however, this fourth phase is truly destructive, and the goddess is truly the evil, devouring hag, the threat to her son, since the son's life (his stagnant form) has to be sacrificed to atone for her cycle of birth and death. Of course, by the model of the One, both are sacrificed back to maia, their common source.

In the ancient myths of the ages of the world, this aspect was known as the Iron Age, when sons were not safe from mothers, friends were not safe from friends, and the entire world was on the brink of total disaster, by either a cataclysmic flood or a fire. In short, the "form" of the world cycle was degenerating back into its chaotic state. Of course, the implications in ancient times was that this occurred in order that the world would once again begin anew; however, we, as modern readers with a linear conception of time (as opposed to the cyclical time of the ancients), erroneously see this phase as Armageddon, the final, decisive battle. In actuality, without the dissolution of every existent form, the hope for the return to the perfection of the One is an unattainable goal; hence the destructive phase.

The goddess in this final phase is the crone, the woman beyond the age of childbearing, the mirror of the virgin in her negative (that is, dormant) phase of creativity. She is once again androgynous, as is the virgin; however, she now becomes identified not with the absent feminine creative One, but with the absent *male* consort with whom she had created her son. Thus, this is a cycle of total death and dismemberment. The son has to return back to his mother for there to be any hope of regeneration; however, their union is impossible because the soil is no longer fruit bearing. The result is that both the son and the crone must be sacrificed back to the One, the original mother (of which the crone is merely a reflection, as the son is the reflection of the father, the sun). These are the myths of Kali, the devourer of men; of the hunters being dismembered by the goddess in the mountains; of the savior sons being hung upon the crosses of materiality; of the universal floods and universal fires, the cosmic equalizers.

As the last vestiges of the old cycle fade into the black night, and the shades of all manifested forms bewail their unhappy fate of returning to the darkness of the moon, only the worshipers of the triple goddess sit together quietly, in the darkness, confidently awaiting the reemergence of the cosmic mother.

Vestiges of the Lunar Cycle

The use of the lunar paradigm continued and was transformed as various mythic retellings of the original experience of the triple goddess. The vestiges of this original lunar paradigm are evident in virtually every hero myth, as well as in myths of male mortals or demigods who perform sacrifices eternally in the underworld. The Greek myths are replete with such examples; the names of the characters reveal startling clues as to the origins of the themes of their tales. Examples of moon goddesses who are involved with heroes include Alcmene ("power of the moon"), mother of Heracles; Semele (from *Selene*, "moon"), mother of Dionysos; Io ("moon"), mother of Epaphus; Pasiphae ("she who shines for all"), mother of the minotaur ("moon bull"); Europa ("full moon"), mother of King Minos ("belonging to the moon"); Jocasta ("shining moon"), mother and wife of Oedipus; Phoebe ("bright moon"). Then there are the lunar males of myth: Menander ("moon man"); Endymion ("seduced moon man"); Ixion ("strong moon man'); Menelaus ("moon lord"); Orion ("moon man of the mountain"). There are also numerous references to the moon as maia power ("insight," wisdom), the most famous of which is personified in the goddess Metis, mother of Athena, whom Zeus swallowed whole when she was pregnant with his child. He reputedly did this because an oracle told him that if Metis gave birth to a son, the son would overpower him, taking over Zeus's function as lord of the sky and earth (again reflecting the lunar cycle).

It is also interesting that this mythic vestige occurs in many non-Greek sources as well: Almah ("moon woman"), Hebrew; Zemelo (Cybele, "moon incarnation"), Phrygia; Nana ("moon"), mother of the savior Attis, Uruk; Chimalman (mother of the Aztec savior, Quetzalcontl); Hina ("moon"), Polynesia. Even the famous Chaldeans of antiquity reflect this cycle: their name means "moon worshipers."

In short, the mythic phase of the fourfold path of creation (maia, mythos, mimesis, and logos) is verified in these voluminous retellings of the same maia experience of the lunar cycle.

The mimetic phase of our lunar paradigm is evidenced by the birth of ritual reenactments by the people of this universal lunar cycle, for their purpose of uncovering that "as above, so below": as the lunar cycle begins, transforms, grows, and dies only to be reborn, so do all things, including ourselves. Thus were the mysteries born, and myths of the earth and water, vegetation, agriculture, and finally eschatology. And with the birth of these rituals came the birth of logos.

In the original lunar paradigm, the logos is the savior son; the "form" created by the opposites (sun and moon) in a re-creation (mimetic expression) of the return to unity (maia). His number is four, because he represents the fourth level of creation (manifestation); the four elements (all of which must be returned back to the One); the four cardinal points (that is, he has geometric existence). Thus, in myth, Hermes is the logos of Maia; Buddha is the logos of Maya; Heracles is the logos of Alcmene; Dionysos is the logos of Semele; etc. The duty of these deities is to serve as "mediators" between the divine and mortal realms, because although they exist in form, their rightful constitution is divine, and therefore they represent the example of the power of maia made "flesh." Their functions then are as dying/rising deities or as psychopomps, messengers that lead the mortal souls to their immortal origins. Taking this lunar model logically, eschatological systems were developed about the compositions of individual humans as divine sparks, emanations from the original flame of maia, and the "form" of the solar father. It was imagined that the stars were fields of souls waiting to return to the mother at the end of the world cycle. Thus Orphism was born, and other mysteries of personal salvation.

The logos phase of this cycle, complete with all the interpretative baggage of the mimetic phase, replaced the simple image of the original cycle of the moon with a complicated diagrammatic process of outlining how mixtures of the four root elements (the proportions of which determined the "form") became mingled into one another in the ever-changing mortal, sublunar realm. Myths of transformation were born: of men turned to wolves or birds, women to plants or spiders, and so forth. Myths of astral characters and hierarchical systems began: how stars were the highest form of things because they had the purest light (sunlight), and therefore only the very noblest of men (heroes) could be deified (made stars). Myths of the afterlife (like Cicero's *Scipio's Dream*) depicted elaborate systems of astral purification through layers of purgatorial spheres in which the soul becomes "pure" of the grosser elements (those that do not shine as well as the sun). In short, this eschatological system allowed for the permanence of the eternal, separate existence of the

original "savior deity" of the lunar myth, by introducing apotheosis, in the form of becoming a star: a permanent image of
the exaltation of the original father, the *form* of the sun.

Finally, with the paradigmatic shift from orality to literacy, the justification systems of theology and philosophy were
born (logos at its best), for the sake of maintaining the validity
of the system in power: the almighty hierarchy of forms. But,
of course, this is the subject of another book.

The Path Back to One

What can be said about the One except that it creates by
dismembering itself,[18] lending its entire being to its created
forms? Only in *this act* can the One ever know itself. Yet, by
this very act of dismemberment, the One loses its essential
unity and becomes transformed into varied physical manifestations, ever changing, though ever retaining the "seeds" of
that original unity, through every re-creation of dividing itself. In short, the only way for the One to recollect itself is by
re-creating that primal desire of the original One to create
Two.

If all of life indeed comes from the One, then each part
of life necessarily contains these seeds of re-creation within its
own form.[19] If we, as parts of the whole, desire to achieve harmonia with our origin (the One), and if we take as given the
fact that actions alone are what determine our relative affinity,
then in order to return to the One, we must follow the
method by which One created the world, namely, the practice
of dismembering the self. This is the essential tenet of
mysticism.

Mystics practice spiritual alchemy to rediscover the divine self, the "One within." Through the practice of such exercises as meditation, they gain the capacity to transform their
bodies, the material "part of the whole," into conscious unity.

The ultimate goal of this activity for them is the complete transformation of all material form into a *conscious* One.

To practice dismemberment[20] (any form of meditation) requires the belief in the model of the One and the understanding of the affinity of the parts to the whole. Once this is affirmed, then the reeducation of the bodily sensorium is practiced (through meditation), in order to ready the "part" to receive the "all."

Mythology is the study of the models—the memory points—necessary to build a self that can carry within the human body all of the acts of all of the gods, in a way that allows the individual the freedom and capacity to always choose the best from among the possible. Remembering that knowledge, in this model, is received *through the body,* as experiential revelations, *not through the appropriation of data,* one should realize, therefore, that there is no information to be found in mythology. All the discoveries will be found in your own bodies,[21] through the dedicated practice of the worship of all the gods through your own living, moving temple.

> Let us with tuneful skill
> Proclaim the Origin of the gods,
> So that in future generations these origins
> May be seen, when these songs are sung.[22]

Chapter II 🌺

Chaos to Cosmos

Cosmology

The themes of chaos and cosmos pervade all myth, yet in their purest forms, they are seen as the two necessary forces in the creation of the universe; therefore, the best place to begin analysis and description of these forces is in myths of creation.

First we must establish the underlying purpose of creation myths, for the modern reader may understand these to be ancient "primitive" explanations of how the world began, pseudoscientific stories told by humans before sophisticated scientific theory set the record straight. This interpretation is a gross error of modernity; nevertheless, without a suitable counter-explanation, modern readers happily persist in this false presumption, especially because myths of creation are rarely considered among the body of knowledge necessary to score successfully on the College Boards.

If creation myths are not designed to explain how things began *in the beginning,* then why are they called "creation myths"? If the answer to how things began is not found in creation myths, then where is it found? If the ancients did not know (or care to know) what happened in the beginning, what is a creation myth? These are a few of the questions that might be asked by the curious reader. It is hoped that these and other questions shall be answered in the following paragraphs.[1]

The purpose of myths of creation is to uncover and recollect how all of creation operates, from the unfolding of the universe, to the development of the community, to the life of the individual. Creation is not seen in terms of historical precedence; therefore, questions like "What happened in the beginning?" are truly irrelevant. The emphasis in creation myths, as in other myths, is on the "how" of things—here, specifically, on how creation is possible. The ancients were concerned not just with what happened before or after the cosmic "bang," so to speak, but with how that occurrence manifests itself throughout all of life.

Unlike our system of time, which is linear and therefore has both a beginning and (eventually) an end, time for a myth-making culture was, for the most part, cyclical.[2]

This basic distinction of time delineation between myth-making and modern cultures can cause us confusion about these creation myths. Therefore, it is best to bracket our notion of linear time for a moment, in order to grasp the fullest meaning of chaos and cosmos as they relate to the act of creation.

For ancient humans, all of existence, all of life, was based on the eternal struggle between the forces of chaos and cosmos. This struggle represented the only time coordinates. The universe, the agricultural cycle, the rise and fall of communities, the development of the human body, the perfection of the soul, the generations of the gods, were all viewed somewhere within this chaos/cosmos continuum, and the only certainty in life was that these two forces were universally operating. Every myth takes for granted these invariant forces, and in myths of creation, especially, their manifested images become clear.

Chaos[3] (Gr. gap, yawning) is the realm of undifferentiated possibility, the "One" out of which the universe is born and to which the universe eventually returns, only to be reborn, the realm of both death and immortality, the source from which all manifested forms originate and to which all forms eventually return. It is the primordial womb, containing the seeds of all things, yet no thing in form. It is the eternal whole.

Cosmos[4] (Gr. ordering) is the name given to any manifested form that "springs" from the primordial womb of potentiality. Since it is only part of the whole, it is temporal, that is, it is born, exists, and dies; it is the realm of the changeable; it is ever escaping, and from the moment of manifestation, it is falling back toward its source (chaos). It is the force of action, insofar as it is constantly in motion. All of material existence necessarily falls into the realm of cosmos.

Myths of creation seek to evaluate and recall this ever-flowing movement from chaos to cosmos to chaos, and certain descriptions of these forces appear as universal images, cross-culturally. It is a mistake, however, to focus merely on these images without regard for the actions being performed on or by these images. This is the error of so many myth theorists: cataloging the myths by images without emphasizing their respective functions. What needs to be shown is how these images are moved in the myths, and what functions these images have in relation to the other actions performed in these myths.

Creation myths usually begin by describing the realm of chaos.[5] Sometimes chaos is viewed as a darkness or a watery abyss, containing a conglomeration of everything in the universe, but undifferentiated:

> When above the heaven had not yet been named,
> And below, the earth had not yet been called by a name;
> When Apsu primeval, their begetter,
> Mummu, and Tiamat, she who gave birth to them all,
>   still mingled in their waters together,
> And no pasture land had been formed and not even a
>   reed marsh was to be seen;
> When none of other gods had been brought into being,
> When they had not yet been called by name and their
>   destinies had not yet been fixed . . . (*Enuma Elish*)[6]

> Then there was neither existence nor non-existence,
> Neither space nor the sky spreading beyond;
> What moved, where? In whose protection? Was there
>   water, unfathomable, deep?
> Then there was neither death nor immortality, nor any
>   sign of night or day.
> Breath was then, without air, by self impulse of the One,
>   other than that there was nothing beyond.
> Darkness was concealed by darkness with no separating
>   sign,
> All was water in chaos. (10.129)[7]

> Before land and sea and sky overhead,
> All nature was one appearance, enclosed in a circle,
> They called it chaos, a rough and disordered mass con-
>   taining nothing but stagnant weight whose seeds
>   inharmoniously together were heaped. (Ovid, *Meta-
>   morphoses*, lines 1–9)[8]

The important thing to focus on in these descriptions is the emphasis on potentiality rather than actuality, inaction rather than movement.

Chaos can also be represented as the whole from which the world is created. It is the womb matrix of time immortal, since it possesses the possibility of all of creation:

> From the whole are all things, all things form a whole, all things are one, each part of all, all in one; for from a single whole these things came, And from them in due time will one return, that is ever one and many. . . . For so undying death invests all things, all dies that's mortal, but the substrate was and is immortal. (Linus, *On the Nature of the World*)[9]

Occasionally chaos is viewed as the dark reminder of death, since eventually all things return to it in order to become re-created as another cosmos, in another time cycle. For this reason, chaos is also imagined as the primordial dragon who covers up the possibility for movement; as the snake who devours things whole yet remains forever new, shedding itself of itself in rhythmic cycles; of the three-faced goddesses who give birth, allow life, and then force death at their whim, as this description of the goddess Kali-Ma recalls:

> You are the original of all manifestations; you are the birthplace of even us; you know the whole world, yet none know you . . . you are both subtle and gross, manifested and veiled, formless, yet with form. . . . Resuming after dissolution your own form, dark and formless, you alone remain as One ineffable and inconceivable . . . though yourself creator, protector and destroyer. (Mahanirvanatantra)[10]

This is perhaps the greatest human revelation; that immortality and death are manifestations of the same force.

Cosmos is the primordial "scream of individuation," the bursting forth from the security of wholeness to assert boundaries and the other, the willful act that takes form. Cosmos is the realm of action, the time in this eternal cycle to appropriate movement, to gain experience, to induce transformation. Since it is the realm of the changeable, it is necessarily also the realm of illusion; thus, manifestations created in this realm of cosmos are always subject to the reverse effects of their actions: decay, ignorance, and mortality.

Once actions begin and a cosmos is generated, that cosmos necessarily falls victim, by its very action, to the realm of chaos. Yet all that can be done in the realm of cosmos is to act: inaction proves to be a graver misdoing, as it immediately heralds in the force of chaos in its most destructive manifestations, and the cosmos that wanted so strongly to remain becomes destroyed by its very own desires. Knowledge of this dilemma is the essence of the tragic worldview of the heroes.

The creation of a cosmos out of chaos is usually depicted as any activity that *forces open by acting upon* the primordial unity. Thus the separation of the earth and sky constitutes the first cosmos:

> Earth and sky were one; but upon their separation from each other they brought forth all things, showing them up to the light, trees, birds, animals, fish nourished by the salt tasting sea, and the race of mortals. (Euripides, *Melanippe the Wise*)[11]

> The original make-up of the universe had the earth and the sky as one single unity, their natures indistinguishable; but [in their separation] two bodies appeared away from each other, and the cosmos appeared as we see it. (Diodorus)[12]

Other activities representing the creation of cosmos out of chaos include the castration of a father by his son, the bursting forth of a creator deity from the cosmic egg, and the dismemberment of a dragon, snake, or other beast by a mythic hero or deity. Each of these actions causes the dissolution of the preceding cosmic order and simultaneously marks the beginning of the new era, under the leadership of the victorious actor:

> for water was the origin for the totality of things, according to (Orpheus), and from water, slime was established, and from both of them was generated a living creature, a snake with a lion's head growing on to it, and in the middle of them the face of a god, Heracles and Chronos by name. This Heracles generated a huge egg, which being completely filled by the force of its begetter burst into two through friction. So its top part ended up as Ouranos, and the underneath part as Ge; and a certain double-bodied god also came forth. And Ouranos having mingled with Ge begets, as female offspring, Clotho, Lachesis and Atropos (the Fates). (Athenagoras, *pro Christianis*)[13]

Finally, something must be said about how cosmos becomes created out of chaos, if by definition chaos is an inert force. There are several accounts of how this original motion/countermotion of chaos and cosmos came into existence, but the most universal response to this question in myth is the presence of the heat of desire (Greek, *eros;* Sanskrit, *tapas*). Desire is the force that links together the cycles of chaos and cosmos while retaining none of their respective attributes in itself. It is the bridge that allows one to flow into the other, though its rightful position is with neither side. Plato best describes this peculiar role of Eros in the following passage from the *Symposium:*

He is neither mortal nor immortal. . . . Neither in
need nor without need, his place, moreover, is mid-
way between ignorance and wisdom.[14]

It is only through desire that one can at once apprehend time
in a single vision, in its perpetual motion, while inhabiting
one side or the other of the chaos/cosmos continuum. For this
reason desire plays a crucial role in the spiritual quest of
mythic man. After all, it is through desire alone that creation
is made possible; eros is that pivotal force that breaks open the
chaotic realm creating worlds:

That one, that had been covered by the void,
Through the heat of desire (*tapas*) was manifested.[15]

Sacred Marriage (Hieros Gamos)

The sacred marriage is the paradigmatic union of opposites that yields the creation of the immortal progeny: gods,
monsters, giants, nymphs, and the like. It is imagined as the
union of the earth and sky (a symbolic return to the chaotic
realm of potentiality) in a cosmic act of procreation.

The lofty sky passionately longs to enter the earth,
desire overcomes the earth to achieve this union.
Rain from the sky lover falls and impregnates the
earth and she brings forth pasturage for mortals
and flock and Demeter's harvest. (Aeschylus)[16]

The sacred marriage also represents the ideal union, the
perfect creative act of forming a cosmos out of chaos. Thus,
each human act of creation was viewed as a repetition of this
original, divine union, thereby restoring the universality of
the forces of chaos and cosmos operating in the world.

The gods are the progeny of the sky and the earth. They spew forth from that space opened up by the separation of these two regions. This is why in myths of creation the gods are born later than the cosmos:

> Who can here say ... from where creation came?
> The gods come later, with the creation of the universe. (10.129)[17]

> And Gaia first of all brought forth an equal to herself, Uranus, the starry heaven, to cover her about on all sides and to be an ever certain dwelling place for the blessed gods ... (when) she lay with Uranus, she bore deep-eddying Oceanus, Hyperion, Iapetus, Theia, Rhea, Themis, Mnemosyne, the gold-crowned Phoebe and lovely Tethys. After them the youngest was born, the wily Cronus, the most dreadful of her children, and he hated his vigorous father. (Hesiod, *Theogony*)[18]

The sky is usually personified as the Indo-European weather god who rains upon the earth, who breaks open the cosmos with the forces of lightning and thunder and infuses the dormant earth with creative energy. The sky deity is the active force in this sacred union, the agent of transformation, the male sexual force.

> Let me sing what Indra did,
> The first deed the thunder wielder performed.
> He killed the dragon, released the waters,
> He split open the side of the mountain.

> He killed the dragon hiding in the mountain:
> His thunder-bolt Tvastar made for him;
> Like cattle lowing their calves,
> The waters rushed, roaring and tumbling to the sea ...

Indra, when you killed the first-born of the dragons,
You uncovered all that lay hidden:
You created the sun, the dawn and heaven . . .
Indra with his powerful and deadly thunder, dismem-
    bered Vtra, most powerful dragon.(1.32)[19]

The earth is personified as the primordial mother goddess who receives the seeds of immortality and brings them
forth as manifested forms. She is the receptive force, the universal womb and personification of all that is feminine:

The different from us all, the oldest, the hard, shining
    rock,
Whatever lives of the land, she is the one to nourish it, I
    sing to the Earth.
Whoever you are, in whatever manner you come upon
    her sacred ground,
You of the sea, you that fly, she is the one who nourishes
    you, she out of her bounty.
She gives birth to beautiful harvests, to beautiful
    children,
Life itself she gives, life also she takes away, all our lives
    are hers . . .
Now mother of the gods, lover of the sky . . . farewell.
    (Homeric Hymn to Gaia)[20]

The forces of chaos and cosmos are implicitly designated
to this pair: chaos to the earth mother and cosmos to the sky
father; however, in the individual act of the sacred marriage,
a larger vision of the chaos/cosmos continuum becomes
evident.

When the sky and earth join together, it is a re-creation
of the return to chaos, a symbolic return to the origin from
which both were separated. When the pair separate, a cosmos
is restored and the gods are born.

In many accounts of the sacred marriage, the sky deities become jealous of their created progeny and attempt to destroy them by either swallowing them or stuffing them back into Earth:

> The children born of Gaia and Ouranos... were hated by their father from the beginning. As soon as each of them was born, he would hide him away in the depths of the earth and would not allow him to return to daylight. (Hesiod, *Theogony*)[21]

> Rhea was joined in wedlock to Cronus and bore him glorious children.... Great Cronus swallowed these children as soon as each one came forth from his mother's womb, having this purpose in mind; that not any other one of the illustrious gods should have the honor of being king among the immortals. (Hesiod, *Theogony*)[22]

These acts by the sky fathers represent an attempt to stop movement, for they realize that the creation of another cosmos (in their children) simultaneously heralds their own destruction. The acts of swallowing or hiding the children inside earth are another example of the return to chaos.

In these myths, following the paternal attempt at stopping the flow of cosmos, they (the sky fathers) become victims of their own actions. They eventually are overthrown by their sons, who take their place in the cosmos:

> Mighty Uranos came, then, carrying night with him, he lay over Gaia with the passion of love all stretched out; his son stretched out his left hand from its knot, took the huge jagged sickle in his right hand and quickly cut the genitals from his father's body to cast them behind him. (Hesiod, *Theogony*)[23]

Gaia laid into the arms of Cronos . . . a large stone
wrapped in swaddling clothes. He, then, placed it
down into his stomach. . . . He did not realize . . .
that his son, victorious and free, had been kept alive
instead of the stone. . . . In time, great Cronos . . .
gave birth again to his offspring vomiting up first
the stone he had swallowed last. It was Zeus who
set the stone firmly upon the earth . . . as a sign. . . .
He also freed his father's brother . . . whom his
father had bound tightly. . . . With trust in these
he rules over mortals and immortals. (Hesiod,
Theogony)[24]

The acts of castrating one's father, or battling one's father, represent the victory of this new cosmos over the old
world order (represented as the father). Of course, once the
new hierarchy is established, this cosmos too will necessarily
repeat the same cycle as the prior one, and the new sky father
and earth mother will be eventually overthrown by the force
of chaos, only to be reconstructed as a new cosmos by *their*
children. Such is the eternal struggle.

Generations of the Gods

With each *hieros gamos* a new generation of gods is
born.[25] These gods are created in that space of separation between earth and sky; therefore, their mythical abodes are usually somewhere between earth and sky, though not in either
realm: mountaintops, ziggurats, treetops, the ocean encircling
the earth.

Usually the gods are generated in groups: twelve for the
Greeks, nine for the Egyptians, thirty-three for the Hindus of
the Rg Veda. Within each of these generations, one pair is
viewed as the representatives of the sacred marriage. Thus, in
Hesiod's account, Ouranos and Gaia are replaced by Cronus

and Rhea, who are replaced by Zeus and Hera. The peculiarity of the Hesiodic system is that this transference of roles stops with Zeus, because of his ingenious way of handling his own destiny of being overpowered by his children. The results of Zeus's activity yield the beginning of mortal time and the creation of a mortal cosmos.

As the myth goes, the first wife of Zeus was not Hera but Metis. When Metis became pregnant, Zeus swallowed *her* whole, so as not to run the risk of being overthrown by his own children, as was done to his father by him and his grandfather by his father.

In the meantime, Zeus and Hera were married, and Hera produced a child without the aid of her husband (similar to the way Gaia produced Ouranos). That child was Hephaestus. Hephaestus ultimately became lame, either because Zeus hurled him out of Olympus in disgust or because he was born that way. Nevertheless, he is personified as the divine craftsman, the blacksmithing god, the one who takes what already exists in material form and re-creates it. He rarely, however, creates from "nothing."

One day Zeus came to Hephaestus complaining about an awful headache. Hephaestus took his trusty axe in hand and broke open Zeus's head. Springing out of the void was the goddess Athena, full grown and dressed in armor.

Athena, child of Zeus and Metis, is the embodiment of her mother's attributes of cunningness and mental agility coupled with her father's military prowess. She is a virgin, female deity, however, thereby insuring Zeus's immortal reign.

Hephaestus cutting open Zeus's head with an axe represents an attempt at creating a cosmos out of chaos. (Zeus swallowing Metis represents the original chaotic act here.) Since Hephaestus is a deity more closely linked with transmutation than actual procreation, and since the axe was hurled to release not the procreative energies, but the mental faculties, in Zeus, the results of the activity are ineffective. Athena and Hephaestus, the next rightful pair of the sacred marriage, will never repeat the sacred act of their forefathers, and therefore at least this cycle (of creating gods) stops. The union of their attributes, however, heralds in the creation of a mortal cosmos, where the exercising of mental faculties and the introduction of the imitative arts take precedence over the creation and generation of gods. This is the end of the age of immortality and the beginning of the world as we know it.

Creation of Man

There are several myths of the creation of man and the various races of man. Hesiod's version perhaps stands as the most popular, if not the earliest or best, account:

First, the immortal gods . . . created a Golden race of mortal men. They lived in the time of Cronos . . . like gods, free at heart, without toil and sorrow. They knew no old age . . . only good things happened to them . . . and [they] were loved by the gods. . . .

But when the Earth came in contact with this race, the gods on Olympus created a second race, a race of Silver, inferior by far, not similar to the Golden race in might nor power of mind. . . . They could not control violence and hate among themselves, nor did they sacrifice to the immortal gods or service them. . . . Zeus was angered by them. . . . But when the Earth came in contact with this race, Zeus . . . created a third race of humans, out of ash trees, a race of Bronze, not similar to the Silver race, they were full of fear, yet strong, busy with war and violence. They ate no bread and had hearts of steel. . . . They had great bodily strength, and their arms were unbreakable. They made bronze weapons, and houses and tools of bronze. When these people destroyed one another with their own hands, they went into the dark and icy home of Hades and into oblivion.

But then the Earth also made contact with this race, and Zeus . . . created one more race, the fourth upon the rich earth, a race even more stubborn and militant, an imitation of the gods' race called a race of heroes or demigods. These were our ancestors through the whole earth. These people destroyed themselves through horrible wars and terrible battles . . . death covered them, but Zeus . . . brought others to settle at the corners of the earth, a life and living place apart from human kind. They live distant from the immortal gods, Cronos is their king. They live with free hearts on the isles of the blessed by the deep, swelling Sea, these are blessed heroes for whom the earth bears sweet fruit, with three harvests every year.

I wish I did not have to live among the men of the fifth race, the race of iron, men who only toil and labor by day and collapse by night. The gods pour on them endless suffering, though some good fortunes come to them mingled with bad ones. Zeus will also destroy this race of mortals. (Hesiod, *Works and Day*)[26]

Ovid offers the following account of the creation of man:

What thus far was absent from this world arrangement,
An animal closer to the hearts of the gods,
Possessing capacity, intellect, reason,
To maintain this kingdom, to dominate earth.
Whether from seeds of immortals did that artisan forge
    him,
That one who fashioned the rest of the world,

Or the seed of Iapetus (Prometheus), molding the fresh
    earth,
That newly had severed itself from high aether,
While retaining still, the seeds of the gods,
And mixed with rain water, Prometheus sculpted man
    into the likeness of all of the gods. (Ovid, Metamor-
    phoses)[27]

The creation of woman is described by Hesiod in much
the same way as Ovid chooses to describe the creation of man.

Hesiod offers two different accounts of the creation of
woman. The reason why woman was created in the first place,
however, remains the same: as a punishment for mankind, due
to the fact that Prometheus stole fire from the gods to benefit
man.

According to the myth of the creation of woman found
in Hesiod's *Works and Days,* woman was formed by Hephaestus by mixing water and clay together into the image of an immortal goddess (similar to the way Prometheus sculpted man
in the account given by Ovid, above). Athena taught her how
to weave; Aphrodite gave her grace, and longing and cares
that bring pain and weariness to the soul and body; Hermes
gave her a shameless heart and a deceitful disposition. She also
was given a jar containing different sources of misery to mankind, "a plague to men who eat bread," which she opened, releasing these hardships onto the earth. Thus, although before
the creation of Pandora "the tribes of men lived on earth re-
mote and free from ills and hard toil and sicknesses," after she
let loose these troubles upon the earth, this Silver race of men
came to an end.

The account in the *Theogony* of Hesiod offers an interesting variation of the myth of Pandora, the first woman.
Here Pandora was created solely by the deities Hephaestus
and Athena:

Zeus caused evil for men, as the price of fire;
the ... limping god [Hephaestus] made out of
earth the figure of a shy maiden. ... The shining-
eyed Athena girded and clothed her with orna-
ments of silver, and from her head down she spread
over her a broidered veil. ... She covered her head
with a beautiful crown of gold made by the very famous limping god's own hands. ... It was wonderful to see, for of the many creatures from the land
and the sea, this was the most ornamented, with
wonderful things and even a voice: great beauty
shone for all to behold. ... And wonder overcame
the immortal gods and mortal men when they saw
what was pure deceit, never to be overcome by men.
(570–90)[28]

Finally, the last race of man was created, according to
Ovid, by the daughter of Pandora (Pyrrha) and the son of
Prometheus (Deucalion). In this account, Zeus decides to destroy the race of humans by a flood, and all are killed except
Pyrrha and Deucalion. At the advice of Themis, they are told
to repopulate the earth by throwing the "bones of their
mother" behind their backs. Deucalion interprets this to mean
to throw stones, and so they each in turn hurled stones over
their shoulders; those that Pyrrha threw became women,
those thrown by Deucalion became men. And so the earth
was repopulated with a new race. In addition, the couple conceived a son, Hellen, who became the father of the Greeks
(Hellenes).

To recap, then, the Golden race of man, which lived under the reign of Cronus, seems to have been created more on
the order of nymphs and the like as opposed to truly mortal
humans. The Silver race of man was the one with which Zeus
became enraged because they refused to offer proper sacrifice
to him. This is the race that received from Prometheus the fire

of the gods, and that was given Pandora as retribution. Pandora is the mother of the Bronze race of man. (Epimetheus is the father.) This is the race produced by Hephaestus and Athena. Hesiod's heroic race was produced as a result of Zeus's various affairs with the mortal women of this Bronze race. Finally, the Iron race was created as a result of Pyrrha and Deucalion's acts of throwing stones over their shoulders. This race, since it was "begotten without love," was a hard, crude race. Nevertheless, through the loving union of Pyrrha and Deucalion other members of this race were conceived (the Hellenes), so the hardship was mitigated by some good.

Perhaps the most interesting race of man for our purposes is the heroic, for Hesiod's introduction of this race, which breaks the metal imagery of the entire myth, has irked mythographers for years. In actuality, however, it is the presence of this heroic race on the earth that saves Zeus's plan of creation in the universe, for without it, mankind would simply remain the mere simulacra of deity, the embodiment of nothing but the image of sheer guile, like their mother, Pandora. Through the race of heroes, who are the human manifestations of deity (since they are born of both divine and mortal elements), mankind can once again return to the age of perfection, albeit after generations of hardship on the earth. This preserves the hope for the continuity of existence, by the repetition of the divine acts of procreation in the human sphere. Further, the hope for a blissful afterlife is possible, under the reign of Cronus (who reigns over the Golden Ages), as opposed to being mere shades in the dark realm of Hades. Thus the mortal-bringing actions brought to humanity by the progeny of Hephaestus and Athena (deceit, craftiness, and false image-making based on external images from the created cosmos) can be overcome by the infusion of immortal acts as performed by the heroes in imitation of divine models. This is the beginning of the path back to perfection.

Ages of Man

The degenerative pattern of the successive races of man evidenced in the myths of Hesiod can be incorporated into a larger myth scheme: the ages of man. Generally speaking, myths of the ages of man repeat the pattern of cosmos to chaos through the recounting of the rise and fall of humans, with each newly created race falling short of the capacities of the preceding one. This cycle of degeneration, however, when it reaches the point of complete anarchy (i.e., an Iron Race), returns by its own destruction into the primal abyss of chaos and eventually becomes reborn as a new cosmos, marked by the return of the Golden Age.

This concept of cyclical time, which has already been discussed in relation to myths of creation, can be seen as the ancient method by which certain generations can be separated from other generations; as the time markers, if you will, of existence in the ever flowing, eternal movement of chaos and cosmos.

There is a correlation between the races and ages of man, and myths of both seem to correspond with one another in their descriptions of these races and ages.

By far the most important age is the Golden. It is marked by the first act of individuation: the creation of a cosmos from the realm of chaos. The Golden Age represents the world at its best, the cosmos at its apex:

In the beginning the age was Golden,
When all men practiced faith and virtue.
No laws were fixed on tablets of Bronze,
No suppliant crowds were fearing their judges,
for men lived safely without this protection.

Not yet had any pine tree been cut down,
From mountaintops, hurled into waves of the ocean,
To set sail in order to come upon foreign worlds.
Men were content with coasts of their own.

Towns were not yet surrounded by trenches steep,
No horns of bronze were blown, none straight nor
   curved,
Nor were there soldiers or helmets or swords,
For people enjoyed peace and tranquility.

Untouched by the rake or wounded by plowshare,
The land itself produced and offered man willingly,
Red mountain strawberries, fruitful arbutus and
Mulberries clinging to bramble bush, tightly,
And acorns from Jupiter's wide spreading oak.
Spring was eternal and warm peaceful Zephyr
Caressed all the flowers produced without seeds.
Next, even corn was produced from unplowed land,
And unfallowed fields turned white, burdened with
   grain.
Soon rivers flowed with milk, streams flowed with
   nectar
and out of the green oak tree dripped golden honey.
   (Ovid, *Metamorphoses*)[29]

The essence of immortality spews forth from this description: eternal spring, crops produced without toil, streams
flowing with nectar (food of the immortals). This is the
mythic realm of paradise, the place of perfection, of the time
of innocence, of before the "fall"; it represents the nostalgic
past when everything was perfect, the dawn of culture.

The cycles of the ages are marked by certain natural phenomena that occur with certain regularity, thereby allowing
set patterns to be established in these myths. Basically, myths
of the change of cycles from Gold to Silver to Bronze to Iron
are marked by alternating myths of universal floods or universal fires. The myth of Pyrrha and Deucalion cited above re-
counts one of these events. Plato's myth of Atlantis[30] might
also be considered among myths describing the culmination
of an age of man, as would the myth of Phaethon, son of the

sun deity Helios, who attempted to drive his father's sun chariot but instead began a cataclysmic conflagration upon the earth.

Plato explains the reasoning for these natural phenomena of floods and fires in the following passage:

> There have been, and will be again many destructions of mankind arising out of many causes; the greatest have been brought about by the agencies of fire and water. . . . [The myth of Phaethon] really signifies a declination of the bodies moving in the heavens, around the earth. (*Timaeus,* 22c–d)[31]

This brings us to an interesting factor determining the ages of man; that is, the relationship between the movement of the heavens and the cycles of ages. In general, myths recounting the return of the Golden Age, marked by the *Magnus Annus* (Great Year) are heralded by a special alignment of the celestial vault, a return of the stars to their original ordering.

Each culture scientifically calculated this great event to occur, though none agreed as to the number of human years it would take for the complete revolution of the cosmic ages. The ancient Hindus, whose myths of the ages of man were described in the four yugas, calculated the time as follows:

> The Great Year (*Maha Yuga*) is calculated to return every 4,320,000 years. The cycles, or ages of man are divided as follows:
>
> > Krta Yuga (Golden Age) .... 1728,000 years
> > Treta Yuga (Silver Age) 1296,000
> > Dvapara Yuga (Bronze Age) 864,000
> > Kali Yuga (Iron Age) .... 432,000[32]

The Chaldeans, who calculated the Great Year to occur every 432,000 years, believed not only that the astronomical cosmos would return to its original position, but that actual events on earth would repeat themselves, exactly as they had done before. In later times, the Stoic, Neoplatonic, and Neo-Pythagorean sects adopted this view of the Great Year, though it was calculated to occur every one thousand years. This belief was probably based on the description of time offered in Plato's *Timaeus:*

> Time, then and the heaven came into being at the same instant in order that, having been created together, if ever there was to be a dissolution of them, they might be dissolved together.... The sun and moon and five other stars, which are called the planets, were created . . . in order to distinguish and preserve the numbers of time.... That there might be some visible measure of their relative swiftness and slowness as they proceed in their courses, God lighted a fire, which we now call the sun.... Thus then . . . night and day were created, being the period of the one most intelligent revolution. And the month is accomplished when the moon has completed her orbit and overtaken the sun, and the year when the sun has completed his own orbit.... The perfect number of time fulfills the perfect year when all eight revolutions, having their relative degree of swiftness, are accomplished together and attain their completion at the same time, measured by the rotation of the same and equally moving. (*Timaeus,* 39a–d)[33]

To conclude, then, the concept of cyclical time, which seems to have been verified by the ancients through the study of astronomy, stands as the cosmic image of the forces of chaos and cosmos. Each cosmos, or age cycle, completes its rotation and then returns to the origin, only to be re-created as a new cosmos, a new age.

Conclusion: The Spindle of Necessity

It is interesting to describe the comparative narratives of creation myths and uncover certain consistencies among them; nevertheless, several questions still remain. Why were these myths constructed in this manner? What is the underlying structure that grounds all myths into these seemingly cohesive systems, as described in the preceding pages? What is the model that provides the necessary and sufficient criteria for this form of narrative transmission? In other words, why did the myths *have* to be transmitted the way they were transmitted?

The answers to all of these questions are found in the study of ancient acoustics: the musical/mathematical model that formed the epistemology of all oral cultures, of which myth is a part.[34]

The acceptance of the orality of mythic transmission is almost common knowledge, and this is not at issue here; rather, we choose to describe the particular methodological procedure for "reading" myth through the musical criteria by which it was constructed, by first describing the operative epistemology of oral culture.[35]

The groundbreaking discovery of the model of sound as the epistemology of oral culture was first outlined by Antonio de Nicolas, in his philosophical study[36] of the ancient Hindu text, the Rg Veda. Since this text is one of the oldest of India's sacred works (composed about 2500 B.C.), its existence alone sheds much light upon our own study of the historical pervasiveness of the mythic tradition. More importantly, however, is the knowledge we derive from de Nicolas's (and McClain's, after him) methodological system for the understanding of the complex reading of these works by their own musical criteria.

As we have alluded to in the Introduction, there are two epistemological methods for deriving meaning in our world: the literal and the oral. Simply, the literal model focuses on objects, nouns, things within the time/space continuum, and creates worlds through the focus on substances as the building blocks of existence. *Knowledge* is, therefore, derived in this model through the appropriation of information about the nature and categorization of substances.

The oral model is based on the relationships among actions, the focus being not on substances but on perspectives. Knowledge, in this model, is achieved by revelation through the embodiment of actions as experienced through the training of the individual.

Since our culture has embraced the literal model, to the virtual exclusion of the oral, we seem to have universalized the former epistemological approach as the *only* human foundation for the acquisition of knowledge, and as a result, the interpretation of myth has become a theoretical free-for-all. The following analysis of myth, through the oral criteria of music, is an attempt to return myth to its proper, rightful abode.

The Musical Model

The best method for describing how the epistemology of oral culture operates is by using the musical correlatives in that system, since music itself is the scientific verification that grounds this epistemology.

De Nicolas[37] examined a fourfold system of relationships that occurred in the Rg Veda, which provided the linguistic key to the musical model. Basically, all of the hymns followed a fourfold scheme consisting of these acts: nonaction (Asat), action (Sat), sacrifice (Yajna), and embodied movement (Rta). These four actions correspond to the four musical acts of dividing the musical string to create tuning systems. Asat represents the uncut string; Sat is the act of cutting the string; Yajna is the giving up of one tuning system for another; Rta is the harmony of the musician with the realm of all possibilities embodied in the string: the union of the singer with all the songs. The linguistic correlatives of these languages is as follows: Asat is the dragon, who must be slain for anything to move; Sat is the act of the mythic deity, cutting open the dragon to release the world; Yajna is the repeated action of breaking open dragons, performed by the heroes; Rta is the reminder of the necessity of repeating this cyclical motion from inaction to action, as it guarantees the immortality of the universe.[38]

The Greek creation myths can also be analyzed on this model. Chaos can be equated with the realm of Asat; cosmos is the realm of Sat; Yajna represents the acts of generating the gods through the *hieros gamos;* and Rta is the cyclical path of the universe as evidenced in the myths of the ages of man.

This very rudimentary association between these Greek myth paradigms and the model uncovered in the Rg Veda merely serves as an appropriate starting point for our investigation of the influence of this musical system of Greek myth, by offering a cohesive argument for the *necessity* of the structure of the myths as presented in this chapter.

In the next chapter we shall explore the realm of the Olympian gods, using this musical model as a guide, to show that their genesis, placement, and overall functions reflect the fact that the Greeks were indeed operating with full knowledge of this epistemological worldview, as a possible source for the creation of worlds. In fact, the importance of studying Greek myth in particular is that it encompasses *both* models in its system, for the Olympian pantheon is constructed in such a way as to assure that both worldviews remain alive within the sphere of human embodiment.

Chapter III 🌿

Models of Perfection: The Gods and Goddesses

Perhaps the most important thing to address at the outset, when discussing the gods and goddesses of the Greeks, is to distinguish their position in culture from that of our Judeo-Christian conception of deity. As has been shown in the last chapter, the gods of the Greeks, and of most myth-making cultures, are born *after* the creation of the world; therefore, they cannot in any manner be compared with the patriarchal omniscient, omnipotent, creator God of Judaism or Christianity. In fact, the primary function of these deities of myth-making cultures is not to make moral judgments about humans, nor is their position to impose dogmatic rules of behavior. Rather, the gods of a myth-making society stand as models of perfection toward which each individual human may aspire. Each deity personifies particular acts by which the entire culture is carried forward. Each deity is venerated (as opposed to adored) through the exercise of the individual while performing the acts associated with that deity. Since all the deities *collectively* form the model of perfection *in a culture,* they all must be equally worshiped.

In a system containing a plurality of deities, one might be inclined to impose on it some hierarchical or chronological guide for interpreting *particular* acts of the gods within the myths, in an effort to provide some static structural foundation to the seemingly endless morass of names and relationships. Both of these approaches are simply invalid and virtually impossible, specifically because deities both replicate as well as duplicate actions often associated with other deities, and at times, acts of particular deities seem to even contradict themselves. For example, the goddess Artemis is the patron of both the hunter and the hunted beast; her brother Apollo is the god of both medicine and plagues. Seen in the more cosmic sense, of course, one recognizes that these are both deities of equilibrium; therefore, their relative actions are directly in response to the particular circumstances with which they are faced at any given time. Thus, the best method of interpreting gods might be by focusing on acts performed rather than on the actors, so to speak. The particular gods manifest only as certain types of actions under certain conditions; they are not entities fixed in stone, but flowing channels of energy that manifest through whatever forms allow their expression.

This leads to the final issue in comprehending how worship of these gods is practiced. To properly venerate these deities is to know when and under what circumstances to call upon them. That is, at any given time, one must be aware of what actions need to be performed, in order that the situation be resolved successfully. This requires that the individual be well versed in all the acts of all the gods, so that when the opportunity arises, one is able to choose the "best act from among the possible acts," as Plato says at the end of *The Republic*. This is the primary training, the goal of education, and the mark of true wisdom for these cultures.

What follows in this chapter is a guide to the gods of the Greeks, based upon the acts they perform and the realms from which they arise. The examples shall come primarily from what is commonly referred to as the "Olympian pantheon," though wherever relevant, other deities shall also be examined.

Zeus, Poseidon, Hades: Male Space Markers

Zeus, Poseidon, and Hades are the three sons of the Titans Cronus and Rhea. According to Hesiod, after Cronus had eaten five of his six children (all but Zeus), Rhea, with the aid of her parents, sent the baby Zeus away and replaced him with a rock in swaddling clothes, which Cronus ate, thinking it was the child. When Zeus grew to maturity, he fed Cronus an emetic (given to Zeus by Metis), causing Cronus to vomit his children, in reverse order. It is for this reason that Hestia and Zeus are both considered the oldest and youngest children of Cronus and Rhea. With this act, Zeus's brothers, Poseidon and Hades, were released.

Soon after, these brothers were allies in a war against the Titans. When Zeus and his brothers triumphantly won the battle, after ten years of fighting, they cast lots for the joint rulership of the universe. Zeus received the sky, Hades received the underworld, and Poseidon was allotted the sea. The earth and Olympus were jointly ruled by all three. In gratitude for having saved them, all the gods and goddesses also granted Zeus the supreme rulership over the affairs of gods and men.

Origin of Olympians (Hesoid)

| | Ge | Earth |
| | Ouranos | Sky |

Aphrodite (from foam)

Cyclopes
Ash Nymphs
Giants
Hekatonkeires
Titans—Cronus-Rhea

		Hestia
		Demeter
	Hephaestus	Hera
		Hades
		Poseidon
	Athena	Zeus—(Metis)

Zeus-Maia	Zeus-Semele	Zeus-Leto	Zeus-Alcmene	Zeus-Hera
Hermes	Dionysos	Apollo	Heracles	Hebe
		Artemis		Ares

Olympians and Their Functions

Zeus	—Thunder wielder, rules heavens
Hera	—Marriage, childbirth
Demeter	—Grain, mysteries at Eleusis
Hades	—Underworld
Poseidon	—Water, horses, earthquakes
Hestia	—Hearth, center of the universe, virgin
Athena	—Wisdom, strategic warfare, crafts (weaving), music, virgin
Hephaestus	—Blacksmithing, demiurge
Aphrodite	—Sexual love
Hermes	—Commerce, messenger, communication, patron of merchants and thieves
Dionysos	—Wet vegetation, wine, mysteries
Hebe	—Cupbearer for the gods, keeps gods immortal
Ares	—Bloody war
Apollo	—Medicine, music, plagues

Artemis   — Protectress of wild animals and hunters, virgin
Heracles   — Paradigmatic hero

Zeus[2] is the prototype of the Indo-European sky god. His name is derived from the Indo-European root meaning "to shine." He is the cloud gatherer, the storm bringer, and the one who pours forth rain from the sky. His symbol is the thunderbolt, and he had been associated with the Babylonian storm bird, Zu; the Hindu gods Brahma and Indra; the Roman Jupiter. In his capacity as sky father, he performs the *hieros gamos* (sacred marriage) with his sister/wife Hera to create divine beings, and with various mortal women to generate the race of heroes on earth. Through myths of his childhood, especially during the time when he was hidden on the island of Crete, Zeus's myth narratives form the basic "trials and sufferings" paradigm that marked the destinies of the subsequent race of heroes. Thus, his myth acts are twofold: he is the prototype fertility sky god, as well as the archetypal hero.

As the one who releases his siblings from the bonds of chaos (within his father's belly), Zeus becomes the "creator/orderer" of the new cosmos of Olympians. He is the one who sets the boundaries of their spaces and, as such, assumes "rulership" over their actions. As Hestia's mirror image (now the oldest, now the youngest), Zeus is the first manifested deity of the Olympians *after* their release from chaos (Cronus), thus he generates the subsequent *manifestations* of the One, divided now into a cosmos.

Hades,[3] whose name probably means "unseen one," is best known as the god of the underworld. His Roman counterpart, Pluto, is known as the lord of wealth, presumably of the hidden treasures beneath the bowels of earth. His primary associations then seem to be as both a fertility deity as well as the personification of the realm of the dead. Judging from one of his epithets, "Zeus Katachthonios" (Zeus of the underworld), Hades seems to represent the sky god in his second phase, that is, as the "god hidden within the earth." He, like

Zeus, is associated with horses and cattle, two universal symbols of male sexual prowess.

Hades rarely left the underworld, and due to his rather ominous position as lord of the dead, very few myths are associated with him. Perhaps the only significant myth involving Hades is how he acquired his wife, Persephone.

Persephone is the daughter of Zeus and Demeter (goddess of grain). One day while Persephone was picking flowers, Hades, in his four-horse chariot, broke through the earth and kidnapped her, plunging the poor girl into the underworld to be his bride. All of this was done with the approval of Zeus but not of Demeter. After much difficulty, Demeter forced Zeus to let Persephone free, which he agreed to do. Unfortunately for Persephone, however, Hades had tricked her into eating seeds from a pomegranate (food of Hades); as a result, she was forced to spend a portion of each year with him in the underworld.

In later myth, *Hades* became the name given not only to the god of the underworld, but to the underworld region itself. Mortals who had died were received into Hades's realm as mere semblances of their material forms, destined to perform the same tasks that they had performed on earth, but without feelings of pleasure or pain. This is the fate that awaited the race of mortal creatures on earth; eternal action devoid of sensation.

Poseidon,[4] or Roman Neptune, rules water and is associated with bulls and horses. Some of his epithets are "nurturer of plant life" (Phytalmios), "earth possessor" (Gaiechos), and "horse god" (Hippios). A further epithet, "earth shaker" (Enosichthon/Ennosigaios), also attributes to him the power of earthquakes.

The origin of his name is not certain, though it appears on Linear B tablets in the feminine, *Poseidaia*. Some have connected the first part of his name with water, thereby justifying his association with the sea. Others have interpreted the root *potei-* to mean "lord." As to the meaning of the second part of his name, one can only conjecture. Some say it means earth, thus Poseidon would be *lord of the earth;* others contend that it refers to Zeus, thereby making Poseidon another aspect of the sky father.

His symbol is the trident, a three-pronged weapon that he uses to pierce the earth and bring forth the waters. His wife is Amphitrite, a minor sea deity whose name means the "all-encompassing triad." Though it is difficult to say from the Greek accounts alone just what Poseidon's function is among the pantheon, a look at his counterpart, Shiva, in Hindu mythology may reveal an interesting focus.

Shiva[5] is one of the manifestations of the Hindu trinity (Brahma, Visnu, Shiva) that mates with the triple goddess Kali. In his manifestations as Shiva, the god carries a trident, is associated with bulls and horses, and is responsible for bringing forth the growth and fruitfulness of vegetation. Among his epithets are "he whose form is water" (Jala-murti), "bearer of the Ganges" (Ganga-dhara), and finally "Lord of the universe" (Visva-natha). Most importantly, however, is Shiva's primary action as the cosmic dancer, who controls space and time through the movement and rhythm of manifested form. In this capacity, Shiva is the cosmic "earth shaker."

Comparing for a moment the Hindu trinity of Brahma, Visnu, and Shiva to the Greek trinity of Zeus, Hades, and Poseidon, one can begin to comprehend the function of the acts performed by these deities. Like Zeus, Brahma represents the lord of progency (Praja-pati), the cosmic patriarch (Pita-maha), and the supreme ruler (Paramesthin). Visnu may be compared with Hades, for both are the "dark ones," the "bearers of fortune," the "pervaders." Finally, Shiva and Poseidon represent the eternal procreative flow through cosmic movement. In short, each of the three represents a single phase in the universal act of creation. From the standpoint of myth, they personify the models of male procreative energies as channeled through various transformations, divine and mortal.

Hestia, Hera, Demeter: Female Space Markers

Hestia, Hera, and Demeter are the three daughters of Cronus and Rhea, who, according to myth, were swallowed by their father in an attempt to destroy them. When Zeus fed Cronus the emetic, these three were vomited back into existence, with Hestia manifesting last, though technically she was the oldest of Cronus and Rhea's children.

There was an old saying among the Greeks, "To begin with Hestia," and so they did. Hestia,[6] whose name means "hearth," was the goddess who received the first offerings at all the sacrifices to the gods, for she was revered as the most venerable among them. Though precious little is known about her, specifically because little reference is made to her among the myths, she is nevertheless an important goddess whose relevance is sometimes underplayed.

Most of our information about Hestia comes from the Homeric hymns, where we are told that she is both the oldest and youngest child of Cronus and Rhea, and that she is a virgin, though both Poseidon and Apollo sought her hand. Because of her vow of chastity, Zeus made her the most honored of all the gods. The Homeric hymn to Aphrodite explains Hestia's unusual position in the pantheon as the one who sits in the hearth receiving the choice offerings.

Hestia, as goddess of the hearth, occupied the central position in both the household and the community. The household hearth was the pulse of the family unit, just as the public hearth was the mystical source of the city's welfare. Nowhere was this more the case than in Rome, where the temple of Vesta (Hestia's Roman counterpart) was the most cherished among sacred abodes.

Hestia's rightful abode among the gods and humans was in the central regions of things. On earth, this sport was Delphi; among the Greek islands, the spot was Delos; and in the cosmos, her home was in the uppermost atmosphere, the realm of fiery aether. As guardian of the divine flame, Hestia later became known as the protector of this divine aether, which was the "insight of the gods and goddesses." Thus, in her essential capacity for human understanding, Hestia personified enlightenment and true knowledge. She is the flame that animates humans and gods and goddesses.

Given this, it is no wonder that few myths of her exist. As the one who gives insight, she certainly would not be a participant in the activities of those in the manifested realm, for her part in the scheme of things is to be the "source from which" all things flow, as opposed to one of the manifested forms among those things created. In this sense, Hestia personifies the force of chaos in the Olympian pantheon, since only through her is the comprehension of other things possible, though strictly speaking, she embodies no thing.

Hera[7] is the "rightful" partner of Zeus, that is, the personification of the female earth goddess in the *hieros gamos*. She and Zeus replace their parents, Cronus and Rhea, in this function. (Cronus and Rhea replaced their parents, Ouranos and Ge). As the sister/wife of Zeus, Hera's primary function seems to be the model of womanhood, the personification of the stages of the feminine life cycle. She is first and foremost the goddess of marriage, and secondarily the mother of Zeus's children, Ares, Hebe, and Eilythia. Among her epithets, which reflect her role as the model of the phases of woman, are Hera "the complete one," that is, "one who is married" (Teleia); Hera "the maidenly" (Parthenie); and Hera "the widow" (Chera). She is occasionally described as a goddess of childbirth, though this function seems to have passed to her daughter, Eileithyia. She is best known for her relentless struggles against her husband's lovers and children, the most notable among them being Heracles, whose name ironically means "glory of Hera." Seen in the broadest sense, Hera personifies the acts that constitute a wife/parent within this framework. Hera's acts reflect the typical acts of a female *within the household sphere*, developing from a bride to a wife to a widow.

Demeter,[8] whose name probably means "earth mother" or some form thereof, is, in the strictest sense, the goddess of vegetation and grain, though based on her many epithets, she seems to be more appropriately placed as a dying/rising deity, whose function is eternal fecundation through death and regeneration. Demeter is known as the goddess "of the earth and underworld" (Chthonia); as "she who sends up gifts" (Anesidora); and finally as the "bringer of fruit" (Karpophoros). By Zeus, she has a daughter, Persephone, who is married to Hades, lord of the underworld, thus linking her further with the dying/rising model. Demeter's most important action, however, seems to be her establishment of the mysteries at Eleusis.

According to the Homeric Hymn to Demeter, the sacred mysteries were started to commemorate the return of Persephone from the realm of Hades (death). Those who were initiated into Demeter's sacred mysteries were guaranteed the continuity of life after death.

In her maiden aspect, Demeter was simply Kore ("maiden" in Greek); later *Kore* was said to be another title for her daughter, Persephone. It seems that the three, Kore, Persephone, and Demeter, serve to describe the attributes of the ancient triple goddess (Kali), whose three manifestations as creator, protector, and destroyer (virgin, mother, crone) mark the cosmic movement from and to chaos. The mysteries of Demeter would then seem to elucidate to the initiates, through divine revelation, the veracity of this cycle of the universe, and within it, of humankind.

The female space markers, Hestia, Hera, and Demeter, like their male counterparts, seem to forge patterns of existence within the realm of mortal possibilities by offering models of creation within the spheres of divine creativity, mortal procreation, and cosmic generation and regeneration, respectively. Although the creative acts of the male deities are for the most part the same, that they become manifest and how they become manifest are entirely dependent upon the receptive vessel who receives and transforms them.

Athena and Hephaestus: Divine Artisans

Athena and Hephaestus represent the first example of a *hieros gamos* gone bad. The results of their unusual births and subsequent actions lead the universe deep into the mire of materiality and farther away from its divine origins than ever before.

Athena is the daughter of Zeus who sprung out of his head, fully grown up and dressed in armor. She is the result of the union of Zeus with Metis (whose name means "cunning"). Rather than running the risk of being overthrown by his children as his father was by him, Zeus swallowed the pregnant Metis whole. Athena was born when he complained of a headache and Hephaestus, the blacksmithing god, cut open his head with an axe.

Athena[9] is the archetypal virgin, as her epithet "Parthenos" suggests. She is a goddess of strategy in warfare, reason, justice, and wisdom. As Athena "Ergane" (the worker), she is the patron of farmers, weavers, spinners, and other craftspeople. She is also the patron of orators and lawyers, by combining her two areas of influence, thought and craftsmanship.

When Zeus asked Hephaestus to create the first woman, Athena was said to have aided him by clothing her and adorning her head with a golden crown. Thus, Hephaestus and Athena were responsible for the creation of mortal woman, a previously unknown image, albeit not conceived in the usual fashion of the *hieros gamos*.

The natural complement of Athena in the realm of the manifested world is the god Hephaestus.[10] Hephaestus, or Vulcan as he was known in Rome, is the divine artisan who utilizes fire as the primary element in the transmutation of his metals. Though the etymology of his name has not been universally accepted, one interpretation is that its root may come from the Greek word for "to kill a fire." This interpretation would be consistent with his Greek attributes but even more so with his attributes as the Roman fire deity, for the god Vulcan originally was primarily associated with the uncontrolled manifestations of fire, such as volcanoes.

Hephaestus's origin is questionable. According to some accounts he was the son of Zeus and Hera; other accounts report that he was the parthenogenically conceived child of Hera. One of his most recognizable features, his lameness, was brought about because he was hurled out of Olympus when he was a youth, either by his mother or by Zeus. Nevertheless, the deity regained his position among the gods of Olympus in the end.

Aside from his duties as the blacksmithing god, he also was responsible for the creation of the palaces of the gods of Olympus. Zeus often called upon the artistic ingenuity of Hephaestus when the thunder wielder was in a bind; it was Hephaestus who chained Prometheus to a cliff; forged the metal bullets used in the Gigantomachy; molded the first woman, Pandora, out of clay and water as a punishment for mankind; and cut open Zeus's head with an axe, thereby releasing Athena.

Hephaestus was also responsible for many deceptive creations brought about by his own cunning imagination: the golden throne for Hera, which bound her to it; the robe and necklace of Harmonia, which was fraught with curses and misfortune; and most humorously, the invisible net that was hung over his bed, that caught his wife, Aphrodite, and her lover, Ares, unaware. As the deity most proficient in the imitative arts, Hephaestus later became associated with the de-miurge, the creator of the material world. In this capacity, Hephaestus was said to have created the world of appearances, according to a Neoplatonic myth, by forcing the world soul to gaze at itself in a mirror fashioned by the lame god. Thus, his position as the creator of the material, changeable world was established.

In Plato's dialogues,[11] it is Hephaestus who is the benef-icent deity who aided humans in achieving civilization, through his teaching of the blacksmithing arts. As a result of Hephaestus's craft, humans learned to overcome the hostile environment by harnessing the destructive forces of nature for his or her own benefit. As the artistic complement of Athena, Hephaestus represents the whole range of human creation in the imitative arts. He is the deity who takes what already exists in elemental form and forges it into shapes for practical use. Thus, he is not generally regarded as a procreative deity; like Athena, his action is creation through transmutation.

Between the realms of Athena and Hephaestus there exists a third artisan deity: Prometheus.

Prometheus,[12] son of the Titan Iapetus, was reported to have fashioned a race of men out of clay. These men, whom Zeus did not think highly of, were unable to warm or cook their foods, nor could they keep warm, as fire was an element reserved only for the gods. One day, it is said, Prometheus stole the fire of the gods from the smithy of Hephaestus by hiding it in a stalk of fennel and brought it down to earth as a gift to mankind. This precious resource, coupled with the wisdom of Athena and the artistic skill of Hephaestus, seemed, to Prometheus, to be sufficient sources of protection for his race of men. Unfortunately, Zeus became aware of this crime and ordered Hephaestus to fashion a women (Pandora) to be a plague to the race of men. According to the mythic tradition, Prometheus's punishment for this crime was that he was chained, by Hephaestus, to a cliff in the Caucasus

Mountains. Each day, an eagle would swoop down and peck out his liver; each night the liver would grow back again. After thirty thousand years, Prometheus was finally released.

Prometheus had a son, Deucalion, who, together with his wife, Pyrrha (daughter of Pandora), repopulated the earth after the great flood by throwing stones over their shoulders. Some say it was Prometheus who inspired Deucalion to perform this task, thereby being indirectly responsible even for this new race of men.

Many times the functions of Hephaestus and Prometheus are confused, possibly due to the fact that their respective actions are so interrelated. In fact both represent humans' yearning for the capacities of the gods, while simultaneously reminding humans of their inferiority in that realm. Both Prometheus and Hephaestus bridge the division of mortal and immortal by their activities. In their own personifications, they are divine; however, their realms and their primary activities are with the concerns of humans. In fact, their sympathies lean toward humans because humans are the product of the acts of these two deities. It is their divine responsibility to protect their creations from the wrath of those immortals who have little understanding of the plight of the mortal.

Together these artisan deities, Athena, Hephaestus, and Prometheus, provide all the acts necessary to create a material existence. They collectively represent the cognitive and dexterous skills necessary to build a complex society. Their sphere of influence, however, remains only at the level of the imitative arts and rudimentary agricultural and social requirements.

Ares, Hebe, Eileithyia: Progeny of Zeus and Hera

Ares, Hebe, and Eileithyia are the three children conceived out of the union of Zeus and Hera. Though individually they exercise a somewhat minimal sphere of influence within the pantheon (Ares is really the only one who some-times is considered an Olympian), as a group they embody the acts associated with death, birth, and immortality. In short, they are the pantheon's time markers, as the manifestations of all the possibilities of time existence within a cosmos.

Ares,[13] or Roman Mars, is primarily associated with bloody war, destruction, and disintegration. His name simply means "battle" or "war," that is, the actual act of fighting a battle or war. Whereas Athena is responsible for the strategy of war, and Nike is the victory of war, Ares is the embodiment of the destructive aspects of war. Like Zeus, Poseidon, and Hades, he receives horses as sacrifices; he is associated with snakes, vultures, and dogs; and he is always accompanied by Phobos (fear) and Deimos (terror), two of his children.

Aside from his function as the destructive god, Ares is also associated with some aspects of fertility, as an earth god. Some of his epithets, such as "fondler of women" and "god of women," suggest this aspect of his character. Though he never married, he had many amorous liaisons, not the least of which was his infamous entanglement with Aphrodite herself. Their affair produced four children: Eros (love), Phobos (fear), Deimos (terror), and Harmonia (harmony).

Ares was the first being ever to be charged with murder. Since he was acquitted of the crime on the hill at Athens, the site still bears his name, Areopagus.

For all his destructive force, Ares was not known for success on the battlefield. His function rather seems to be the mere *destruction* associated with war. As a fertility deity, he may represent the "destruction of the self" that occurs between birth and immortality.

Hebe[14] is the virgin cupbearer of the gods. She provides them with nectar and ambrosia to keep them immortal and eternally youthful. Hebe is the virgin aspect of her mother, Hera. She was given to Heracles as his bride when he was assumed into the heavenly realm (which might suggest why his name is linked with Hera's).

Little else is known of Hebe; her name simply means "youth." As a time marker, she is the source of immortality, for mortals and immortals alike, as long as her cup remains full with the divine nourishment of the gods, for she is the eternal life spring.

Eileithyia[15] is the goddess of childbirth. She bridges the gap between death and immortality, for she embodies both, through the act of childbearing. Some myths describe her specific function as the goddess whose presence is needed for the child to be born, thus making her a boundary deity of sorts. Her name may be a variant of "eleuthyia" (the coming), which would indicate this aspect of her function.

Eileithyia has no real personality, for like Hebe she merely marks a state of action in time. Thus, little else can be said of her except that her presence was often delayed (usually by Hera) at the births of Zeus's illegitimate children (Apollo and Heracles, to name two).

Taken as a group, these three children of Zeus and Hera encompass the boundaries of cosmos and chaos within the mortal realm of influence. Hebe is god time: immortal and eternally youthful; Ares is mortal time: every action, from conception on, heralds in the onslaught of destruction and integration; and finally, Eileithyia is the only reconciliation of these two opposite forces for mortal beings strictly within the mortal sphere of existence; only through the birth of children is the hope of immortality actualized.

Dionysos and Heracles: Two Suffering Gods

Dionysos and Heracles are two sons of Zeus by (different) mortal mothers. Dionysos is the son of the Theban princess Semele, and Heracles is the son of the Alcmena, the queen of Tiryns. Both of these women were persecuted by Hera. Semele was consumed by Zeus's thunderbolt, due to

Hera's diabolical suggestion that Semele ask to see him in all his splendor. Alcmena was in labor for seven days, because Hera delayed Eileithyia's intervention. When the children of Zeus by these mortals finally arrived, it didn't stop Hera from her vengeance; she merely transferred her energies from mother to child, and both children were equally plagued with her attempts to destroy them.

According to the mythic tradition, Dionysos was the reincarnation of the deity Zagreus, a child of Zeus and Persephone who had been dismembered and eaten by the Titans, at Hera's request. When Zeus found out about this act, he burned the Titans to ashes and recovered the heart of Zagreus, which he ground up and gave to Semele in a drink. Thus, Semele's child, Dionysos, was really the incarnation of the baby Zagreus.[16]

Hera attempted to kill the baby Heracles by placing two deadly snakes in the crib where he and his mortal twin, Iphicles, lay. Much to the surprise of all, the baby Heracles wrestled and strangled both of the snakes with his bare hands, thereby thwarting Hera's plans for his extinction.

Both Dionysos and Heracles represent aspects of Zeus's paradigmatic actions, though each corresponds to different facets of their father's activities.

Dionysos,[17] though always a god in his own right, suffered the plight of the misplaced hero: loss of homeland, distrust by family, reared by strangers and superhuman beings. Like the myths of Zeus in his youth, Dionysos was whisked away and hidden in either the mountains or a cave and reared by nymphs until he grew to maturity and returned to his native Thebes.

Heracles[18] seems to have inherited his father's activity of slaying monsters, an act analogous to overcoming the forces of chaos (represented here as the various monsters). He embodies the sky-god function as he passes through the twelve labors, or earthly time markers. As the husband of Hebe, after his apotheosis, Heracles assumed his father's double as Hebe assumed her mother's double, and the two became the born-again sky god and earth goddess.

What is of particular importance in the myths of these two gods, Dionysos and Heracles, is not so much the stories of their sufferings as their respective victories over death and their resurrections. This is what sets these gods aside from other children of Zeus as well as from mortal beings.

Dionysos is best known as the god of wine, though actually he personifies the life-giving waters that fructify vegetation. Dionysos *is* the fruit of the vine; his followers who partake of his substance become infused with the god's presence (*enthusiasmos*) and, in such a state, *become the god*. He forces his worshipers to lose their own perspectives, and they become dismembered through their loss of a reference point, that is, he causes them to see that their mortal manifestations are illusory, that all that seemed fixed in form is really in a constant flow, like the waters of life that animate even themselves, though they remain completely ignorant of it.

In myth, Dionysos is represented as both the slayer and the slain sacrificial animal. For this reason, he is sometimes wrongly accused of being a destructive deity. In actuality, he only destroys what is stagnant, namely, form, by forcing movement in any direction that will lead the individual out of his or her own little, mortal sphere of reality. The method for losing one's self through the power of Dionysos may include such acts as sexual licentiousness, inversion of the social order, arhythmic dancing, or drama. In short, Dionysos returns individuals to the state of their chaotic origins, where they have to reinvent their entire cosmos; their names, habits, thoughts, and ideals. Then he reminds them of the ultimate temporality of all form, and that only the *flow* of life is eternal and real.

Heracles learns this lesson through the constant exercise of transgressing his mortal capacities while performing his labors. For him, the entire picture was not evident; he earned immortality through apportionments of suffering, which caused him to wear down his sense of self by sheer embodiment of action. Though he was originally born a mortal, his repetition of perfect action without attachment to personal gain led the gods to assume him through the flames of his own funeral pyre, to become one of them.

Dionysos shows the path of immortality through dismemberment of the illusive self; Heracles, through the exercise of action without attachment to the result. Both deities endure the "death" of their biographical attachments to form and remind us that the gaining of immortality is achieved by the sacrifice of the self (an invariant form) to the action that flows through it.

Aphrodite and Hermes: Of Love and Magic

Aphrodite and Hermes personify the "acts made flesh" within their respective realms. Aphrodite,[19] as the goddess of love, that is, of *the act of love,* is the divine manifestation of this highest of actions, within both and mortal and immortal realms. Hermes,[20] who is the master god of illusion and whose function is primarily to transgress space, is the god of travelers, borders (including the borders between the heavens, underworld, and earth), communication (both oral and written), merchants (and thieves), and dreams. Though their individual spheres of influence differ, they collectively represent the essential ingredients to insure the continuous flow from chaos to cosmos: the power of love and the manifestation of that act in fluid form. Quite simply, they are the deities of transformation.

Aphrodite's birth seems to allude to her rather unique position in the pantheon. According to Hesiod, Aphrodite was born when Ouranos and Ge (sky and earth) had broken apart, after their son, Cronus, castrated his father with a sickle. According to the myth, the severed genitals of Ouranos fell into the sea, and Aphrodite was born from the sea foam.

This explains the origin of her name (*Aphros* means "sea foam"). Homer, however reports that the true parents of Aphrodite are Zeus and Dione (literally, goddess), and this led to the distinction offered in Plato and elsewhere of the two Aphrodites, one earthly and the other divine. It seems that the origin of the need to distinguish between the two Aphrodites was in the ancient mysteries, which sought to distinguish the animalistic sexual urge from divine love, both being within the sphere of Aphrodite's influence.

Though Aphrodite was married to Hephaestus, she had many lovers, both mortal and divine. Among her children are Eros (love), Harmonia, Fear, Panic, Aeneas, and Hermaphroditus (whom she conceived with Hermes). Because of her birth, she is associated with the sea, and with such sea creatures as swans and dolphins. She is also the nurturer and protector of gardens, and among flowers, roses and violets are her special varieties.

Hermes is the personification of sheer guile. He is the son of Zeus by the female Maia (whose Hindu counterpart, Kali Ma, created the world of earthly appearances by making things perceptible). His realm is really the world of images, or illusions; therefore he is associated with magic, divination, astronomy, alchemy, weights and measures, and finally, the transformation of elements on the material plane.

According to some sources, the Neoplatonist philosophers associated Hermes with the Logos, or word made flesh.[21] His symbol, the caduceus, was a rod with two snakes entwined around it, and it was said to have represented the kundalini power actualized to its fullest potential.[22]

In mythology, Hermes bridges the gap between the gods and humans by bringing the will of the gods to the mortal realm, through either divination, communication, or action. Since his qualities are at best elusive, it is difficult to pin down exactly what Hermes is capable of doing. In fact, if you think you've pinned him down, chances are you've been duped.

Hermes's number is four, representing the four corners, directions, seasons, elements—namely, anything that appears in manifested form. He is the one who gives space to action, thereby lending it form.

As a pair, Hermes and Aphrodite conceived Hermaphroditus, the androgyne.[23] Here the presence of this child represents the return to unity (the realm of Chaos) through the combined attributes of these two deities. For the Olympian pantheon, they serve as the universal archetypes of manifestation through creation, the knowledge of which assures the continuous flow from chaos to cosmos to chaos. . . .

Apollo and Artemis: Mirror Twins

Apollo and Artemis are the twin children of Zeus by Leto, daughter of the Titaness Phoebe. According to myth, when Hera found out that Leto was carrying Zeus's offspring, she refused to allow Leto any place on earth to give birth. So Poseidon arranged to raise an island from the waters (Delos), and there Leto gave birth to her divine twins, but only after suffering in labor for nine days because of Hera's attempts to delay Eileithyia.

Apollo[24] is the god of medicine and plagues, music, poetry, and prophecy. According to myth, when he slayed the monster Python, he set up his oracular shrine at Delphi, replacing the mother goddess's function as dispenser of oracles there. This act also marks Apollo as a hero prototype. His symbols are the bow and the lyre, representative of his functions, and for the most part he is associated with the healing arts.

In a certain sense, Apollo represents harmonia of all types. Health is harmony of body; music, of soul; and even his destructive aspect is used only to maintain cosmic equilibrium. Later he was associated with the sun, the divine image of Hestia, whose harmonia was said to embrace the whole universe as the harmony of the spheres.

Artemis[25] was the mistress of animals, as her Minoan origins might seem to indicate. She was the patron of both the hunter and the hunted, for her sympathies went always with the weaker under the circumstances. Artemis is the virgin goddess known as "Diana" in Rome. Her symbol, the bow and arrow, reflects her association with the life cycle of all of nature. As the eternal virgin, her natural abodes are places not wounded by the plowshare, namely forests, groves, and mountains.

In later myth, Artemis became associated with the moon, as the natural complement of her twin Apollo. In this capacity she seems to have rule over the mortal destinies of things, now protecting them, now causing their destruction.

Both Apollo and Artemis are equilibrium gods, of sorts. They maintain the harmonious balance of humans and animals, respectively. In their later associations, as the sun and moon, they represent the earthly time markers of generation and decay, not of individuals but of entire species. As the image of Hestia's fire, Apollo represents the eternal manifestation of divine will on earth, through poetry, prophecy, and music. As the image of the "image" of Hestia's fire, Artemis, the moon, governs the changeable realm of becoming; that is, of material form, generation, and decay. Together, they apportion the cosmos with the mirror-imaging of their respective functions in such a way as to provide it with continuity, order, and harmony.

Chapter IV 🌸

The Fourfold Path

The gods of the Greeks were active participants in the daily lives of all humans. Their position was not somewhere up in the sky, looking down upon their mortal creations with an avenging eye; rather they were alive and flowing within the sinews and bones of every mortal creature who chose to allow them the opportunity to make a home within their human space.

Mythology speaks of the cyclical ages of humankind and the cyclical races of mortals, degenerating from perfection (Golden) to disintegration (Iron). As we have seen, this cycle is the inevitable consequence of existence, once the original unity of chaos has divided itself. The gods, as manifestations of space and actions within this cyclical paradigm, likewise become part of this creation. That is, there are particular gods who favor particular spaces within this greater paradigm of the ages of the universe.

We know that the fourfold motif of the ages of the universe and humankind is evident in most mythology. We also realize that what characterize the movement of these cycles are the mirror images of the acts performed by the gods and by humans.

The Golden Age is characterized by harmony and immortality, eternal youth and an abundant and ever flowing source of live energy. The Silver Age introduces the first division, the seasons, and though spring (the season of regeneration) returns, it must be preceded by a season of death (winter). The Bronze Age focuses on further division—namely, the separation of groups of people and the introduction of weapons—used to assert individual theories. Finally, the Age of Iron destroys even the last vestige of the semblance of unity, the earth, by parceling it out among individuals, by plundering into its bowels to steal metal in order to fashion more weapons in order to appropriate more earth; or to use as currency in order to appropriate more objects in order to possess more of the pieces of the splintering unity, on the faulty belief that the more objects one possesses, the closer one is to the whole.

Each of the gods represents a single ray in this spectrum of ages. Since all the gods of Greece were always around, no one particular age, or viewpoint, could take precedence over the others and force the whole into stagnation, even though through the acts of humans, some acts/gods were always favored over the others (hence the ages). By making the gods of Olympus the models for all action, the Greeks were able to keep alive all the human technologies and faculties necessary to keep the culture in motion. The lesson learned from the myth of the ages is that too much focusing on one perspective leads ultimately to disintegration of the whole.

As we have stated, the gods represent certain acts within the universal sphere of human potentiality. The exercise of all these acts constitutes the knowledge of the whole, that is, of the *movement of the whole*. As humans we all face the possibility of our own limitations; however, at times, through our own focused viewpoints, we lose the perspective necessary to actualize our potentialities and become whole. The following chapters outline the fourfold path of human actions, using the criteria of the acts and spaces of the gods within each path. Each path represents individual choices of life paths, and collectively they represent all the choices of life paths, according to this model. That one path is favored over others collectively by humans, attests to the position of the cosmos within the cyclical paradigm of ages.

The Shadow of Existence: The Realm of Becoming

Artemis controls the realm of images. As the moon, she is the image of the sun, the reflected light, the changeable one. As a model, the realm of Artemis is the world of material forms in a cosmos. We have seen that when using the criteria of chaos and cosmos as the ultimate time markers of creation, reality, that is, eternal "being," rests only in the realm of chaos, in the One.[1] Once the One divides itself, we are faced with the fragmented "forms" of a cosmos, each of which carries with it a piece of the whole, but not the unity of the whole. This realm of cosmos is fraught with images that recall the original act of the One dividing itself. Each image, then, is a manifestation of an act in form.

Given this, we can either focus on the material form, creating systems of categorization by imposing definitions, boundaries, classifications, and values to these *objects;* or we can focus on the acts performed, of which these objects are the mere reflections in time.[2] In the realm of Artemis, humans focus on the former.

The two life paths, as described in myth, that fall within the realm of Artemis are what I have termed the "path of materialism" and the "path of humanism." Their common attribute is their focus on manifested form as the sole criterion and goal of action. While the humanist model perceives human form as primary, the materialist extends and embodies this belief in such a way as to create external artificial constructs to aid in the preservation and perfection of these human forms.

The space deities who rule this realm are Hades and Hera.

Hades is the god of the underworld, who receives the dead as semblances of their former images, an appropriate end for those who focus only on form. He presides over the space of the materialist deities, Hephaestus and Athena, the artisans.

Hera is the immortal stagnator; she is always attempting to stop action because she wants things to remain status quo. She presides over the deities of humanism: Hebe, Ares, and Eileithyia, the three gods of the possibilities of human form.

Together these eight deities[3] rule the destinies of the mortal realm, that is, the realm of perpetual change, not because they as immortals choose to control the existences of mortals, but because those mortals choose their lives with these gods as their models.

The Path of Materialism

Iron Age Model

The path of materialism was forged by the children of Athena and Hephaestus. One might recall that these two deities are the Olympian artisans, whose function is to invent tools, methods, and procedures that enable humankind to harness the oppressive forces of nature for their benefit. The children of Hephaestus and Athena, using the acts performed by these gods as models, create new inventions by superimposing particular form on the objects in their existing environments, to suit their varied needs.

The relative worth of this technique is dependent entirely upon how it is used. When applied to agriculture, for example, Athena's introduction of the use of plows or irrigation systems benefited humankind directly, by aiding them in satisfying the basic human need for food. When Hephaestus applied this art to carpentry, this technique likewise aided in the construction of suitable shelter. The use of metals introduced by Hephaestus was beneficial in either of these capacities as well; namely, to forge weapons to kill animals to eat, or to build stronger and more durable homes.

Extending this technique to its limits, one can argue that the use of automated systems of plowing are more effective in the eventual obtainment of food than are oxen, and therefore should be used; and that construction of homes by displacing forests is ultimately more beneficial to the accessibility of shelter for larger numbers of people, and should therefore be done, regardless of the negative effects these acts may have on the environment, for the criterion here for action is not the harmonious integration of all things, but the focused goal of *people fulfilling their own needs.*

By the same standards, Prometheus's introduction of the use of fire as a tool for aiding in the processing of food was beneficial to humans because it allowed for more culinary variety and because cooking made foods more easily ingestable. By extension, the use of ovens increases the benefit to humankind because, while it offers all of the positive qualities for which fire was used, it has few dangerous side-effects. Microwave cooking, using this logic, is perhaps the most effective method of food preparation to date, because it performs all the basic actions of an oven, but is more time efficient.

Athena's introduction of the law benefited people because it enabled them to form groups that joined together under common values, goals, and ideals, while simultaneously instilling a sense of communal justice that protected the rights of all by providing retribution as a deterrent for "the uncivilized few." When Athena took this function of establishing law away from the gods and placed it into the hands of mortals, her intent was to free people from the imposition of outside arbitrariness as it related to their own existences; to allow humankind the freedom to develop without always having to be concerned with reinventing suitable standards for action.

Today courtrooms are flooded because people have transformed these human obligations into a system of rights and are now concerned about how *their rights* are being violated by employers, who require specific employment standards that exclude some, thereby violating their right to choose a profession; by corporations, who pollute the environment with deadly contaminants, denying them *their right* to breathe fresh air; by other individuals, who don't see things exactly the way they do, thereby inhibiting *their right* to impose their own wills.

It is no surprise that Zeus asked that Hephaestus and Athena be responsible for the creation of Pandora, for he requested it with full knowledge of what the result would be. Zeus wanted to punish man by this creation, and this desired effect worked perfectly. Pandora was a conglomeration of all the worst traits of all the gods, except for her physical appearance, which, though lacking substance, was fashioned in the image of a goddess. That "image" of the goddess alone was good enough to dupe mortal men into the mire of attachments and attraction to physical form to the extent that to this day, entire industries are built on it—cosmetics and fashion, to name just two.

One of Hephaestus's most ingenious mortal counterparts was Daedalus, the master craftsman, sculptor, engineer, and inventor. Among his contributions to humankind were the airplane and artificial insemination. What is often missing from our interpretations of these myths is that these myths teach us of the dangers of this one-sided technology. The dangers of flying are that you may attempt to fly too high and be consumed by fire; the dangers of artificial insemination without the foresight to see all possibilities is the emersion of a hybrid human—in myth, the minotaur.

The repetition of this technology, of transmuting nature to suit one's own needs, to the exclusion of all other technologies, creates the human habit of "doing it because we can," without concern for the consequences of those acts in any larger context than our own individual desires. This criterion of action, the satisfaction of our own needs, becomes more and more focused, our needs multiply, our desires become insatiable, until we become victims of our own artificial creations of artificial desires for satisfaction of artificial needs. The more we relinquish control of our human faculties by lending their functions to these "objects created to serve our needs," the less human we become, through lack of human exercise. Since a calculator can add better than my six-year-old can, why not just teach my six-year-old how to push the buttons on the calculator?

This is not to say that Athena and Hephaestus are unworthy of proper veneration. It only serves as a reminder that they alone are insufficient to actualize our own human potential, and at best, they create very shallow humans.

In myth, the children of Hephaestus and Athena become nameless shades in Hades after they die. They roam about the underworld, performing their daily chores as if they were alive, yet they are entirely devoid of all sensation. Imagine spending an eternity repeating the act of pushing a button.

The Path of Humanism

Bronze Age Model

The humanism path is marked by individuals who believe that the perfect human physical body is the highest criterion of worth and the only definition of self; therefore, their ultimate goals are to keep it young, healthy, and beautiful. They are the spa generation, the "pinch and tuck" inventors, the health-food junkies. They are the "you are what you eat" people, the "body beautiful" people, the *Self* magazine people. They are the "quality time" mothers, the "weekend" dads, and the proud parents of latchkey kids.

This human path is governed by the goddess Hera, through her children Hebe, Ares, and Eileithyia. The basic human dilemma brought about by these gods is this one: While we'd all like to remain young and eternally beautiful (Hebe), time disintegrates our mortal form and we age (Ares). No matter how hard we try, our biological clocks tick the hours away toward our ultimate extinction, and we panic. What will become of us? Then we choose to have children (Eileithyia) to assure the continuity of our own existence, since the sole definition of ourselves is our "genetic makeup," so to speak. Once we have achieved this act of "replicating ourselves," we can continue on our path of attempting to stop the aging process; trying to hold on to our prior lifestyles, B.C. (before children); seeking new and better mates by trading in the older models; and at best, living for retirement when we can spend all of *our* time doing whatever *we* want to do, and answering to no one but *ourselves*.

The root of the problem with this model is belief in the false assumption that *we,* as individual selves, are invariant wholes in the scheme of things. On this faulty premise, we deny the movement of the entire universe, to verify our own importance. Like Hera, who was constantly taking revenge on her husband's lovers because of *her* fear of *herself* or *her* children being displaced in *her* existing interpretation of the scheme of things, we attempt to freeze the world, situations, relationships, our bodies, in an effort to control what can never be controlled: the flow of life.

As if it were not enough that we do this in our social selves, today this human path problem has been introduced as a criterion within the fundamental definition of life itself; that is, we as a culture have so embodied this path that we are struggling with such "quality of life versus quantity of life" issues as the death penalty, euthanasia, abortion, genetic counseling, bioengineering, artificial transplants, artificial insemination, living wills, suicide, and "should we pull the plug" situations, to name a few.

If we learn anything from the myths of Hera, Hebe, Eileithyia, and Ares, it is that it is futile to attempt to stop the world just because you want to get off. Hebe is the source of immortality because of the constant flow of life that she pours forth; Ares is destructive because he holds on and refuses to let go of anything. Hera thinks that because she once acted by having children, she now deserves to be eternally rewarded and that her husband should forever applaud her (single) act by bowing to her every desire. Zeus thinks differently. Finally, Eileithyia silently passes over the earth, granting forms to new souls who have never heard of Lamaze.

Divine Harmonia: The Path Back to One

The realm of divine harmonia is the world of action and is ruled by Apollo. Unlike the realm of becoming, which is created by the focus on material forms within the continuum of time and space, this realm is the world of being, of action, of movement. Apollo rules this realm because he is the Olympian embodiment of divine harmony, as the image of Hestia, the eternal center.[4]

Regarding this sphere of harmonia, there is one cautionary note that must be addressed at the outset. That is, in this realm, where action is the primary focus, one must always be aware that the consequence of any action can have two effects, one up and one down.[5] The human paths that emerge from this pattern are likewise divergent; thus one is always faced with two sides to every model within this sphere of influence.

Ironically, this situation is the only source of human freedom within this mythical model. These are the only conditions under which free will can truly be exercised.

Harmonia is the regathering of the dismembered One through the human effort of recreating the acts performed by the One in the first place. Harmonia is the closest any human can get to the unity of the One itself. Harmonia is *sophrosyne*.[6]

The path of the hero marks the first acts necessary to return to the One: the dismemberment of the self and the focus on the action rather than the actor. Demeter marks the spaces of this path, because she is the embodiment of the one who must constantly lose herself to death in order that re-creation be possible.

The path of the mystic is the path of the One made flesh. Its space is marked by Poseidon, because its form is embodied movement, like that god. The deities that represent the models for action within this realm, Aphrodite and Hermes, are merely the names given to the sheer actions they are—love and power (potentia).

The realization of this path can only occur by looking back on your own footsteps of action.

The Heroic Path

Silver Age Model

The heroic path is marked by the gods Dionysos and Heracles. The divine space marker of this realm is Demeter. The primary focus of action in this model is the exercise of shedding one's mortal taints in an effort to unveil the immortal. Demeter marks this space because of her eternal descent and ascent between these two realms. Dionysos shows the path by illuminating the temporality of the sphere of the senses, while Heracles reveals the method to transgress the physical self through the sacrifice of the actor for the action.

Of course, as this is a realm of action, there are always two possible manifestations of each act; therefore, this is also the path of the anti-hero, who uses these exercises in a focused manner in order not to sacrifice the biographical self but to destroy the physical self, in order not to transgress the temporality of the senses but to desensitize them altogether.

Followers of Dionysos are very clever. They have gone beyond the "keeping up with the Joneses" craze and have managed to live without ever tasting a recipe from the *Heart Association Cookbook*. Their only problem is that they recognize that the majority of people, at root, are really not what they appear to be. In fact, they realize that nothing is really as it appears, including themselves. They could be characterized as the type that always seems to be the popular one, though deep down they can't quite recognize that quality in themselves and they wonder if someday it will go away, or if maybe it was never there in the first place. Or they are the bright but self-conscious type; though outwardly they manifest a cool facade, inside they are a nervous breakdown waiting to happen. There are also the self-sacrificing martyr types, who secretly hate all of humanity because their sensitive, vulnerable psyches had been trampled upon one too many times by an Athena or an Ares. The point is, these people who pursue a Dionysian path of action are aware of the temporality of things and people, and seek meaning in life through breaking down their habitual attachments to these things or people.

Our culture is fraught with the downside choosers of this path; namely, people who are correct in seeing the flaws with materiality and humanism, but who turn their awareness into a destructive model of either self-deprecation or, worse, self-annihilation, through the systematic desensitization of their human bodies through the use of drugs, alcohol, sexual transgression, or compulsion. This action produces the exact opposite of the desired effect. It merely accentuates, indeed exaggerates, the original problem, because it focuses more attention on the individuals *themselves* as objective realities *to themselves,* a fact that they can never reconcile. And worse, these individuals create situations where the very objects that they seek to eliminate from their sphere of reality (shallow people and stupid models of life) become their counselors, spouses, or chastisers. This leads to a cycle of escapism that becomes so habitual that the only real way out becomes annihilation.

The upside of this model produces humans who are able to get around the self-annihilation cycle by surrendering their own wills, that is, actions, to some higher source, which immediately relinquishes their self-induced obligations to others and simultaneously diverts attention from their "self" form. They accept what is within their realm of action and take responsibility for it, and they let go of what is not within their realm of action. They do not attempt to convert the world, nor do they let the world into themselves. The problem with the Dionysian type in general is that since they themselves are exercised in action, they naturally attract others who need to feed off of their energy, so to speak. When they (the Dionysians) let these others in, they acknowledge their existence, thereby making *the form of the other* a reality to themselves. Once they create the other, they feel responsible to carry them. This is deadly baggage for a Dionysian. By not letting them in, however, the Dionysian is free to act or not act as situations dictate, without the concerns of self or other interfering.

The Heracles followers are of two types as well.

The negative variety form religious fundamentalist and missionary sects to impose their own beliefs on the unenlightened and lowly sinners or, worse, pagans; they run social programs for the poor and the downtrodden, for personal profit; they picket for worthy causes in order to gain personal publicity. Basically, the downside of the Heraclean model applies to anyone who performs right acts for the wrong reasons or simply with a particular reason in mind. These social do-gooders have bought into the belief that if the outcome appears to be a worthy cause *to the world at large,* they will do it *and be considered great persons,* and go to heaven when they die. The problem with this belief, of course, is that the purpose of the action, thus described, is completely devoid of merit, as it only serves to reinforce the value of the little self who is doing the action. These types ought to be sent back to the pages of the Book they always seem to quote so well and read, "Beware of practicing your piety before men in order to be seen by them" (Matthew 6:1).

The upside of the heroic path is the model of Heracles. It is the model of doing right acts with no other goal than the perfection of the act itself. The rewards gained by the repetition of this practice are also described in that same Book: "I will raise him up on the last day . . . and he shall have eternal life" (John 6:43, 47).

The Mystic Path

Golden Age Model

The path of the mystic is the path of Aphrodite and Hermes. Here the followers are the embodiments of sheer action, without attachments, without gains. They do not act because of, in order to, with the intention of, on the belief that, instead of; they simply act.

The path of Aphrodite is the path of love; not love of, love for, or love because. This love is a mirrorless act: it is the love of the One desiring itself. It is the embodiment of the all within the part. It is the act of love made flesh through love.

Those who travel the path of mysticism through love, love each part of the whole because they love the whole; they do not seek to find the love of God by loving each human, but they love each human *because* they love God. Through the act of love they break open themselves in remembrance of that original act of the One when it divided to make the world, and they share in this creation through recreation.

Those who perform the act of love of, or love for, or love because, do not love. They idolize, contract, or reason, but they do not love. These are the downsides of the act of love. When the act becomes institutionalized, legalized, or deduced, it dissolves into itself and becomes religion, marriage, and law. While these institutions form the foundations of civilization, they are not the criteria upon which to build a spiritual life.

The path of Hermes is the path of the witness. He is the walking, breathing god who wanders around the earth wondering why the devil he ended up here in the first place, and more importantly, how he is going to get out of here unharmed. Like the Dionysian, the follower of Hermes is blessed with the beauty of form as well as the gift of intelligence, two attributes that *he* would hardly recognize as his own, and he marvels at how those other people get by with so much less, while thinking that any of it belongs to them. He beats everyone at their own game, yet he calls no game his own. He can do anything, but he refuses to be reduced simply to what he does. He goes around like a mirror, causing everyone to reflect on themselves, while he averts the reflective snare, ever shining out of his own internal light, and not from the reflection on some stupid mirror.

When he realizes that there is a reason that he was given these gifts, then he aligns his will to action, and great things occur. If he decides that he was given these things because he is great and *deserves* them, then he marshals his troops together and, like the pied piper, leads the willing flock right into his control. This is Hermes the magician, who uses his powers for his own personal gain or, worse, to cause harm to others.

This same Hermes, however, if he chooses to channel this power to benefit all of humankind, can single-handedly change the course of history.

If there are any Hermes types out there, now is the time to act.

Conclusion: The Path Back to Hestia

Our mythic journey thus far has led us through the paths of the Olympians, showing how each sounds a particular tone within the system of human possibilities. Now is the time to regather these fragmented tones in order to recollect the song.

Of all the deities mentioned in the previous chapters, the ones whose actions have thus far not been taken into account are Zeus and Hestia. As you may recall, these deities share a special, reciprocal kind of relationship in myth; each of them is both the oldest and the youngest child of Cronus and Rhea. As we have seen from our model of epistemology (music), this affiliation of Zeus and Hestia corresponds to the special association between the uncut string (Hestia) and the first division of the string (by Zeus): the tone created by Zeus represents the musical octave of the uncut string, which creates the tonal matrix necessary to build the rest of the tuning system (mythically, the space deities). Thus, as the octave of Hestia's referent tone, Zeus is the younger of the children; however, as the first tone in the new system, as marked by creating the octave, Zeus becomes the older of the two.[7]

This musical diversion is examined only to bring about the following point: by extending this musical relationship to its mythic correlative, we see Zeus as the act of divine attunement, and Hestia as the one to which he attunes. By analogy, then Hestia is the realm of chaos in this mythic model, and Zeus, by his action of breaking open the tuning system, is the first manifested form of cosmos, that is *his tuning system.* This is why in myth he is considered the father of the gods.

Following our musical analogy, Apollo is the god of the realm of action in the Olympian pantheon for the following reason: he represents *acts of the body,* which carry the reflective image of Zeus,[8] through the practice of creating tuning systems; and he is the reflective image of Hestia,[9] through the exercise of harmonizing these systems through music. By this analogy then, Apollo is the god of equilibrium, who maintains homeostasis in the human soul, by *attuning human acts with the acts of the gods*. This is done by the dismemberment of the human senses through the practice of imagining. The human body becomes the string, and the exercises performed through acts of will become the music. If the acts are attuned to the acts of all the gods, then divine harmonia is achieved in the individual. This is the closest human expression of receiving the divine while still retaining human form.[10]

As Hestia and Zeus's realm relates to Apollo's, so does Apollo's realm relate to that of Artemis. In the world of becoming, or rather, forms, Apollo becomes the model of action for individuals in Artemis's space, through the forms produced as a result of the actions of those in that realm. That is to say, those in the realm of form, uneducated in the realm of action, model themselves by imitating the forms, ideas, and beliefs of those in Apollo's realm, because of the faulty belief that the *forms represent the criteria of knowledge there*. Thus, these people merely replicate the images of the others without understanding the creative process exercised to make these images in the first place. In terms of the musical model, they are adept at reproducing the notes, but they can hardly be considered creative musicians.

The problem with this view is that, whether or not one *focuses* on them, *actions* alone determine one's form in the mythic model. Therefore, those in the realm of Artemis are as much victims of their own actions as are those in Apollo's realm, whether or not they choose to focus on them. Basically, just as one attuned to the acts of the gods manifests deity, those attuned to the life forms in the realm of Artemis manifest mortal form. Mythic accounts of these types abound; Ovid's *Metamorphoses* is the best compendium. These myths represent humans who, through the repetition of certain actions, become transformed into an animal or object that performs an act similar to the one performed by the human. Ironically, then, even these myths of metamorphosis reinforce the musical model.

The basic analyses offered in the preceding paragraphs are the accumulated treasures of our human past, reconstructed here from the fragmented ruins of human temples in dire need of repair. This mythic model became the philosophical cornerstone of Western philosophy, through the teachings of Pythagoras and Plato; however, without the exercise of seeing the myths through our own sensorium, we can never truly comprehend the messages in either of their philosophies, though we dare to believe that we can.

The next chapter places this mythic model within the context of the Pythagorean teachings and, through them, the dialogues of Plato, both as a testament to the veracity of the preceding model of myth, and as a guide for the resurrection of the true Pythagorean/Platonic training, and with it, the return of the gods.

Chapter V 🌿

Myth Made Flesh:
The Philosophical Models

In this chapter we shall examine the teachings of both the Pythagorean and the Platonic philosophical systems to show that the cultural contexts against which these two systems stand, and the criteria for knowledge to which they both ascribe, are in fact a result of the embodiment of the mythic imagination.

First it must be stated that the above assertion is not a claim that either of these philosophical schools was concerned with the myths per se; rather, the point being made here is that the epistemological model that grounded the mythmaking culture of the Greeks is the same epistemological model that forms the criteria for knowledge in these schools, namely the oral/aural model of music.

The most important evidence that we have in support of this claim is the emphasis that these schools placed on training, on the exercising of the body and soul, as their educational foundation, as opposed to a system of education based on the accumulation of data. Education by training recalls the mythic understanding of perfect action as the embodiment of divine harmony; the capacity to be always prepared to choose, from among the possible, the best.

I am aware that the above observation merely puts forth an interesting path to explore without very tangible evidence at the outset. It is particularly difficult to proffer the evidence *because* of the fact that it is only through the performance of these exercises that one is even able to *see* the path; however, a reconstruction of the Pythagorean practices, and following them, the Platonic beliefs, shall reveal this path with such clarity that few would be able to deny that the model of these philosophers was indeed the paths of the gods.

Pythagorean Model of Education

Because Pythagoras, like many great sages, taught primarily through oral transmission, what has come down to us as Pythagorean doctrine is a series of testimonia reflecting upon contemporary views of the Pythagoreans and a few biographical accounts of Pythagoras the man. For purposes of this discussion, we shall focus on the Pythagorean system of education as described in the *Vitae* of Iamblichus, Diogenes Laertius, and Porphyry.

Pythagoras was said to have chosen his initiates by the following criteria: quick memory; even temperament; proportional physical form, gait, and grace; intellectual tenacity; humility; and most importantly, self-discipline. These human qualities he believed were the necessary prerequisites to a spiritual life.[1]

After being admitted into the brotherhood, Pythagorean initiates were trained in memory exercises, meditation, music theory, ascetic practices for training the will (vegetarianism, vow of silence, etc.), mathematics (geometry), medicine, astronomy, rhetoric, and philosophical dialectic. These exercises were performed in community with others of a similar capacity (as adjudged by the master himself), though as the initiate progressed, he or she would be permitted to commune with those of more advanced learning.[2]

The purpose of this training was to lead the immortal soul away from the mire of materiality and further toward the realm of the immortals, from which it had strayed.[3] *The entire Pythagorean philosophical system was grounded on the goal of the attunement of the immortal soul of the individual with the divine realm of the gods,* whose manifestations could be apprehended in the *harmony of the spheres.*[4] Through his experimentation with the relationship between musical tones and number, Pythagoras scientifically verified this philosophical position, and thereby systematized an educational training that was based on the repetition of all the divine acts of the gods (as discussed in the previous chapters) in an effort to create, through the body of the individual, the same harmonia that was operating the universe. This is the origin of the mystical tenet, "As above, so below." Humankind, for Pythagoras, was a microcosm of the universe; therefore, by replicating the harmony of the universe by attunement of one's parts to the whole, one became one with the eternal and therefore *was* eternal. The gods Hephaestus and Athena were exercised by the study of logic, rhetoric, and oration; Hebe, Eileithyia, and Ares's realm was exercised by the study of medicine, gymnastics, and wrestling. The Dionysian and Heraclean realm was exercised through the various ascetic practices, and by the study of geometry and astrology; while the Hermetic and Aphroditic path was exercised through music and philosophy.

This training extended to professional services, and the Pythagoreans followed the same model in choosing career paths: politics, medicine/householder, priest, sage. In short, the paths of the gods were the paths of the Pythagoreans. Through the embodiment of the mythic imagination, the Pythagoreans preserved, through exercise, all the human possibilities they believed were necessary for the perfection of the soul. Using this training as an epistemological foundation, Plato attempted to recreate, through the dialogic form, *the conditions under which the exercises of Pythagorean education might be illuminated,* in addition to outlining the basic tenets of that system.[5]

Plato's Mythical Divided Lines

The influence of Pythagorean philosophy in Plato is well documented,[6] though at the heart of the matter, few recognize the *connections* among the "information" presented in the dialogues of Plato, the training of the Pythagoreans, and their foundations in myth. A complete unveiling of these connections would require another volume at least; however, for our purposes it shall be sufficient to focus on one of Plato's most famous literary/philosophical passages, on the divided line, from the *Republic,* to at least uncover the (mythic) structural framework of his philosophical methodology. One might well begin by reproducing the passage in full:

> Now take a line which has been cut into two un-
> equal parts, and divide each of them again in the
> same proportion, and suppose the two main divi-
> sions to answer, one to visible and the other to the
> intelligible.... You will find that the first section

in the sphere of the visible consists of images . . . I mean shadows, and the second place, reflections in water, and in . . . polished bodies and the like. Imagine now, the other section, of which this is only the resemblance, to include the animals which we see, and everything that grows or is made. Would you not admit that both these sections of this division have different degrees of truth, and that the copy is to the original as the sphere of opinions is to the sphere of knowledge?

Next proceed to consider the manner in which the sphere of the intellectual is to be divided. . . . [I]n the lower of the two subdivisions, the soul uses the figures given by the former division as images; the enquiry can only be hypothetical, and instead of going upwards to a principle, descends to the other end; in the higher of the two, the soul passes out of hypotheses, and goes up to a principle which is above hypotheses, making no use of images as in the former case, but proceeding only in and through the ideas themselves. (For example), you have heard that students of geometry . . . assume . . . certain hypotheses, which they and everybody are supposed to know, and they do not deign to give account for them . . . but they begin with them . . . until they arrive at last, and in a consistent manner at their conclusions. . . . Although they make use of the visible forms . . . they are thinking not of these, not of the ones they draw, but of the ideals which they resemble . . . and of this I spoke as the intelligible, although *in the search after it* the soul is compelled to *use* hypotheses; not ascending to a first principle, because she is unable to rise above the region of hypotheses, but employing the objects of which the shadows below are resemblances in their turn as images, they having in relation to the

shadows and reflection of them a greater distinct-
ness, and therefore a higher value.

. . . And this other sort of knowledge which reason herself attains by the *power of* dialectic . . . in order that she may soar beyond the world of
hypotheses *to the first principle of the whole;* and
clinging to this, by successive steps she descends
again without the aid of any sensible objects, from
ideas, through ideas, and in ideas she ends.

. . . Now, corresponding to these four divisions,
let there be four faculties in the soul-reason answering to the highest, understanding to the second,
faith or belief to the third and perception of shadows to the last . . . *and these faculties have clearness in
the same proportion that their objects have truth.* (*Republic* bk. 6)[7]

Immediately following this passage in the *Republic* is
Plato's famous allegory of the cave,[8] which reproduces in narrative form the same distinctions set forth above. Retracing
his fourfold path to its base, one can see the four regions of
the gods of myth as discussed in this text. Plato here was attempting to relate, by proportional analogy, the acts of the
soul with manifestations of the respective forms in the material world. This very philosophical approach is Pythagorean
in practice: the essence of the Pythagorean belief system was
that acts of the soul manifested themselves consistently in certain forms. This Pythagorean belief was a direct application of
the musical epistemology that says that consistent relationships exist between musical tones (acts of the soul) and corresponding string lengths (manifested forms). And this
musical statement is the same scientific verification that the
mythic model reflects. Further, the specific divisions in Plato's
divided line exactly represent the realms of the gods as described in chapter 2. If this were not enough, in another part
of the *Republic* (bk. 3), he divides the classes of citizens into

four groups, which correspond to the mythic acts of the gods they represent (Athena and Hephaestus; Hebe, Eileithyia, and Ares; Dionysos and Heracles; and finally, Hermes and Aphrodite, respectively): farmers, craftsmen, and the like; doctors, athletes, and warriors; guardians; and finally, the philosopher king. In discussing the proper education of these classes, he focuses on acts of the soul that again mirror the mythic divisions: the foundational study of gymnastics and music reflects the acts necessary to embody the two realms of Artemis and Apollo. The other studies correspond more particularly with the acts of the other gods within these realms.

Finally, Plato's criticism of the poets,[9] perhaps the most misunderstood and misrepresented of all his tenets in the *Republic,* can be understood only in terms of this mythic model. At the root of the matter, Plato chastises the poets because they, through the misrepresentation of the gods in their work, have inverted the relationship between the models of perfection, which the gods represent, and the acts of humans. That is, the poets, according to Plato, force human acts to be the critera for the model of the gods, and not the other way around. The reason they are doing this is because they have lost the capacity to traverse Apollo's realm of action, *because they have focused their attentions on the realm of form and therefore are adept only in the art of imitation.* Thus his criticism of them has not to do with the poetry per se; *it is that through the poetry, he is made aware that they have lost the human technology with which they were entrusted—the acts of Apollo's realm—and have sold out to the realm of Artemis.* This is why Plato wants to replace the poets with the philosophers: he believes that they will carry this human exercise in their own training, and in this way the gods will not be abandoned.

Actually, the entire *Republic* is a plea for the return of harmonia to the mortal sphere, from the individual to the community. It is only through the re-creation of the conditions under which the *Republic* was written, however, that we as modern readers can ever truly recognize this fact.

Plato uses the same fourfold model of action in the *Symposium*,[10] to address the function of love, in the *Sophist*,[11] to analyze the arts, and in every other dialogue as well.

It would serve the reader well to look at these works of Plato with new, mythic eyes, to discover the extent to which this philosopher uses the mythic worldview. Plato's dialogues serve as the missing link between our literal path of mortality and the oral path back to the gods, by offering the exact criteria and training needed to make all the gods visible once again.

Conclusion 🌺

Recovering Our Mythic Origins

Every culture that has lost myth has lost,
by the same token, its natural power of creativity.
Only a horizon ringed about with myths can
unify a culture. The forces of imagination . . .
are saved only by myth.

—Nietzsche

If there is anything that one can say about the importance of learning the mythopoetic worldview, it's that it certainly forces one to reexamine one's own worldview. In fact,
for many of us it shows us precisely that the beliefs we most
take for granted as being true and foundational are really

nothing more than our own cultural worldview. But the problem, of course, is that without the mirror of the other, we cannot ever know ourselves.

In an age such as ours, when we have reached the supersaturated capacity for ingesting, processing, and regurgitating information—indeed, when we have created machines that can certainly perform this task better than we can—perhaps we as a society of humans ought to reflect for a moment and ask ourselves the following questions: Who or what are the models that have created this cultural focus? What training is needed to succeed in this worldview? Where is this training leading humanity as a species? And most importantly, Do we know why we do what we do, and could we do otherwise if we wanted to?

The response to the first question is that it seems clear that the models that have created this cultural focus, the Zero worldview, began with the scientific revolutions of the seventeenth century and have progressed into the age of materialism in the twentieth century. The response to the second question is that it appears that the appropriation and synthesis of data form the crux of the training necessary to compete successfully in this modern world market. These are the easy answers, which can be figured out even through the criteria of knowledge provided in the Zero model. But without other models for action, how can we, as a species, begin to respond to the third and fourth questions?

Chances are, some theory or another will provide the response, though the theory, in fact, will have no basis in reality, as it will not yet have been embodied. And, of course, if the theory precedes the existence, then the existence verifies the theory, and never the other way around. Further, once we as a species limit our criteria for knowledge to only the sphere of cognitive functions, then, for lack of exercise, we lose our cultural inheritance of the multiplicity of human acts that can be performed and perfected.

The mythopoetic vision, by training the imagination, provides the way out of this morass by offering models for human action and a multiplicity of perspectives of the world. It allows us humans to break down our boundaries of material form and open ourselves to the unity of the cosmos of which we are all a part. It trains us to focus upon the pulsating life flow that joins all forms and is responsible for the transformation of these forms into one another, from the microcosm to the macrocosm. Finally, it reminds humanity of its immortal origins and offers us the wherewithal for the long journey home.

Appendix 🌺
Charts on the Origins
and Spaces of the Gods

The charts contained in this appendix are meant to provide some visual aids to the reader of this book. As is known, Greek mythology is so replete with foreign names that sometimes it is impossible to keep them all straight. In an effort to ease this burden, I have offered charts of the gods, according to the divisions that are discussed in this book.

I have also included two charts of the philosophical methodology of the Pythagorean and Platonic systems outlined in the last chapter. In this form, the relationship between their respective philosophical tenets and their mythic origins is clear.

The Monochord and Ancient Acoustics

According to the testimony of Iamblichus (*Life of Pythagoras*), Pythagoras discovered the laws of harmony and music while passing by a brazier's shop:

> As he was walking near a brazier's shop, he heard
> from a certain divine causality the hammers beating

out a piece of iron on an anvil, and producing sounds that accorded with each other, one combination only excepted. But he recognized in those sounds, the diapason, the diapente, the diatessaron, harmony. He saw, however, that the sound which was between the diatessaron and the diapente was itself by itself dissonant, yet, nevertheless, gave completion to that which was greater sound among them. Being delighted, therefore, to find that the thing which he was anxious to discover had succeeded to his wishes by divine assistance, he went into a brazier's shop, and found by various experiments, that the difference of sound arose from the magnitude of the hammers, but not from the force of the strokes, nor from the figure of the hammers, nor from the transposition of the iron which was beaten.... He returned home and fixed one stake diagonally to the walls.... From the stake he suspended four chords consisting of the same material.... To the extremity of each chord he tied a weight.... The chords were perfectly equal to one another in length, he afterwards alternately struck two chords at once, and found the beforementioned symphonies.... The chord which was stretched by the greatest weight, produced when compared with that which was stretched by the smallest, the symphony diapason. But the former of these weights was twelve pounds, and the latter six. And, therefore, being in a duple ratio, it exhibited the consonance diapason; which the weights themselves rendered apparent.

Pythagoras was said to have discovered the fifth (the first and third chord, forming the ratio 3:2), the fourth, and the third by the same method. It is said that in this manner

Pythagoras discovered the mathematical foundation of music and harmony.

Though it is generally accepted that this account is not an historical one (hammers striking metal in the manner described above does not produce the stated effects), the theory of harmony discovered by Pythagoras is an accurate one. It appears to have been worked out and verified on a monochord.

The following diagram serves as a reconstruction of the basic elements of Pythagorean tuning theory. Its purpose is to elucidate some of the more technical aspects of the musical epistemology.

Note that this model is universal for all oral cultures and is the source and model (epistemology) for all of mythology.

Figure 1.   Pythagorean Tuning on a Monochord

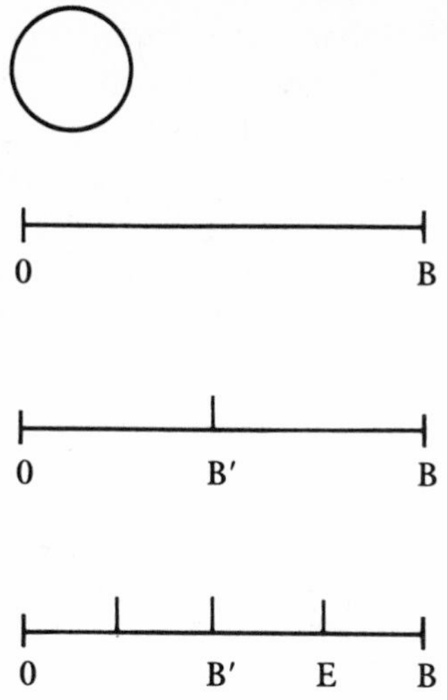

A.   The uncut string. Realm of chaos.

B.   0   B   The string cut and fastened at two ends.

C.   0   B′   B   The string cut in half creates the octave (ratio 1:2).

D.   0   B′   E   B   The string cut in quarters creates; the fifth, B′:E descending (3:2 of)–B′), and the complementary fourth, E:B ascending (3:4 of 0–B).

Figure 1, Continued

E. The rest of Pythagorean tuning consists of dividing the string by ascending fourths and descending fifths. For example, the next tone created would be 3:4 of E (dividing 0–E into fourths), thus creating A. Then 3:2 of A to create D; 3:4 of D creates G; 3:2 of G creates C; 3:4 of C creates F; 3:4 of F creates Bb ;3:2 of Bb creates Eb; 3:4 of Eb creates Ab; 3:2 of Ab creates Db; 3:4 of Db creates Gb; 3:4 of Gb creates Cb. This is where the Pythagorean comma occurs in this tuning system, because Cb ≠ B'.

From Chaos to Cosmos: The Dismemberment of the One

Following the model of the acts performed to cut the string on a monochord, we find that these acts are repeated in what we call the "creation" of the gods. This chart superimposes, on the monochord, the spaces of the gods, beginning with Hestia, who represents the "One" in this model. Each group of gods presides over a particular realm in the cosmos, over an age and race of humanity, and over certain human acts. Together, they form the matrix and the model of the possibilities of the universe.

Figure 2.

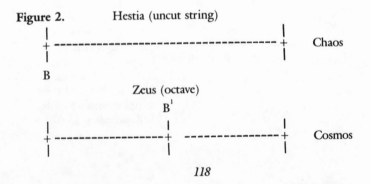

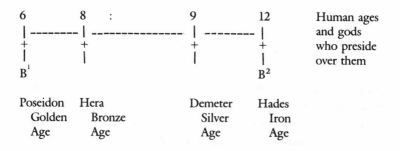

6	8	:	9	12	Human ages
|-------- | --------------- | -------- |					and gods
+	+		+	+	who preside
|	|		|	|	over them
B^1				B^2	

Poseidon	Hera		Demeter	Hades
Golden	Bronze		Silver	Iron
Age	Age		Age	Age

Explanation of Figure 2

On the musical model, Hestia is the uncut string, B. Zeus is created when the string is divided in half to form the octave: the double B'. From that point on, Zeus's realm becomes the area B–B', while the other gods rule the cosmos B^1–B^2. Thus, according to myth, Zeus rules the heavens; Poseidon, the sea; and Hades, the underworld.

Poseidon becomes Zeus's counterpart in the next generation of the gods; Hades is his image: the octave double. Demeter represents the creation of the musical fifth on the monochord, while Hera is the musical fourth, the shadow of the fifth, since the musical fifth automatically produces the fourth.

Together these four gods represent all of the spaces of the cosmos in which humans can function. Zeus appears again in myth only to re-create new generations of gods (in myth, the heroic race).

Membering and Dismembering: Apollo and Artemis and the Technology of Imagining

As we have seen in this text, the realm of Artemis is the realm of forms, that is, the realm of the focus and classification of forms as they appear in whole: human, tree, dog, etc. The realm of Apollo is the realm of action and of *creating forms*, through dismembering the embodied forms of Artemis's realm by lending sensation to create nonexistent *new* forms, on the model of the creation of the gods. Thus, human sensation (i.e., sight, smell, taste, touch, sound) is distributively lent to the forms being made to form the new unities and new sensations. Just as the division of the string creates new worlds, depending on how the string is cut, membering imaginatively is dependent upon the capacity of the individual to divide the biographical unity of her or his own form (by breaking up these sensations as described above) and lending these sensations to create new forms, continuously. This is the path of transformation.

Figure 3.

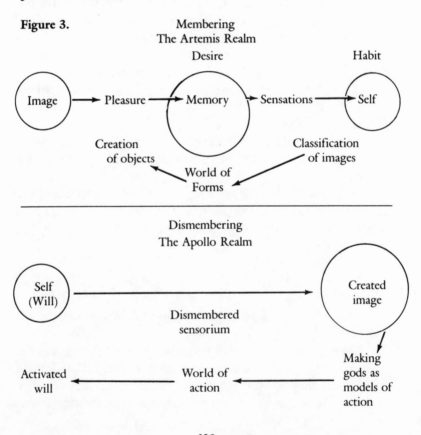

Membering
The Artemis Realm

Desire

Habit

Image ⟶ Pleasure ⟶ Memory ⟶ Sensations ⟶ Self

Creation
of objects

Classification
of images

World of
Forms

Dismembering
The Apollo Realm

Self
(Will) ⟶ Created
image

Dismembered
sensorium

Making
gods as
models of
action

Activated
will ⟵ World of
action ⟵

The One Divided: The Realms of the Gods and the Human Paths

Figure 4 describes the positions of the Olympian gods as they relate to the human paths of materialism, humanism, heroism, and mysticism; in myth, the Iron Age, Bronze Age, Silver Age, and Golden Age. As you can see, the gods operating under the realm of Artemis (creating the material and human paths) focus on material forms (the material being a copy of the human). The paths of humans operating under Apollo's realm, however, focus not on created forms, but on actions needed to be performed in order to induce *transformation* (usually from a mortal to an immortal).

Figure 4.   The One Divided: The Realms of the Gods and the
Human Paths

Realm of Form

Governed by *Artemis*
(Realm of becoming, phases of the moon, the changeable)

Materialism	Humanism
(Hades)	(Hera)
Path of Technology	Path of Individuality

Hephaestus: Blacksmith   *Ares*:   Destruction, war
Athena: Thinking, craftwork   *Hebe*:   Eternal youth
                                          Elythia: Childbirth

Creates simulacra of
material world   Creates mortal progeny

Realm of Action

Governed by *Apollo*
(Realm of "lunar sun," the image of Hestia's fire)

Heroism	Mysticism
(Demeter)	(Poseidon)
Path of the Hero	Path of the Mystic

Figure 4, Continued

Heracles:	labors, misplaced origins, grace for apotheosis
Dionysos:	sacrificed, dying/rising god

Hermes:	magician, son of Maia
Aphrodite:	Eros power

Apotheosis by dismemberment/
recollection through
acts of sacrifice

Fluid transformation
by desire through acts
of will

The Gods and Their Realms (Overview)

Figure 5 is an overview of the spaces of the gods and their roles in the human paths. Note that the god that is chosen to be worshiped by the majority of humans determines the human ages globally, and the god that is chosen to be worshiped by an individual determines his or her own human path. It is only through the worship of all of the gods that immortality is achieved, that being the capacity to create and destroy all forms *at will* and with grace.

Figure 5. The Gods and Their Realms (Overview)

Divine Realm: Deities who mark space

Zeus	Hades	Poseidon
Hestia	Demeter	Hera

Middle ground: Deities who manifest actions and create forms

Artemis   Apollo

Athena	Ares	Heracles	Aphrodite
Hephaestus	Hebe	Dionysos	Hermes
	Eileithyia		

Mortal Realm: Manifestations on material plane

Moon		Sun	
Technological (simulacrum)	Individual (icon)	Heroic simulacrum)	Mystic (icon)
plastic arts	procreation	apotheosis	sheer act
The Realm of Material Form		The Realm of Action	

Pythagorean Training and the Monochord

Figure 6 is an overview of how the mythic model and musical epistemology become fused in the Pythagorean teachings and training. It determines not only the acts performed but also the statements about the world.

Figure 6.   Pythagorean Epistemology

Musical Act	*Mythic Image*		*Philosophical Statement*	
String	Hestia	•	The One	(Chaos) unlimited
Octave	Zeus	• •	The Monad	(Cosmos) limited
Tuning system/5th/4th	Space markers	. . .	Number 3	(Action) Geometrical images
Tuning by major 3rds	Middle-ground gods	. . . .	Number 4	(Manifestation) Form

Pythagorean Training for Harmonia

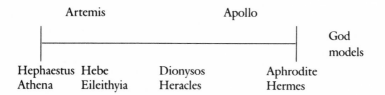

God models

| Hephaestus | Hebe | Dionysos | Aphrodite |
| Athena | Eileithyia | Heracles | Hermes |

Figure 6, Continued

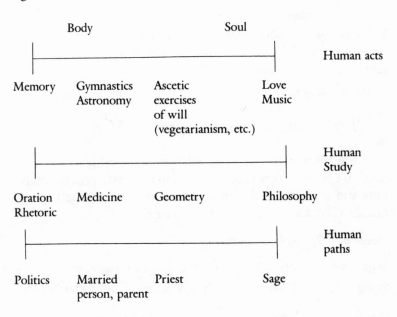

Plato's Mythic Divided Lines
==

Figure 7 is an overview of the whole Platonic corpus, through its main dialogues. It is obvious that the model of music as epistemology is the one Plato wants to preserve through philosophy, since the poets had failed in this task.

Figure 7.

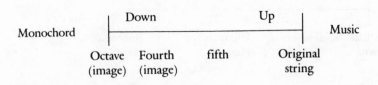

Figure 7, Continued

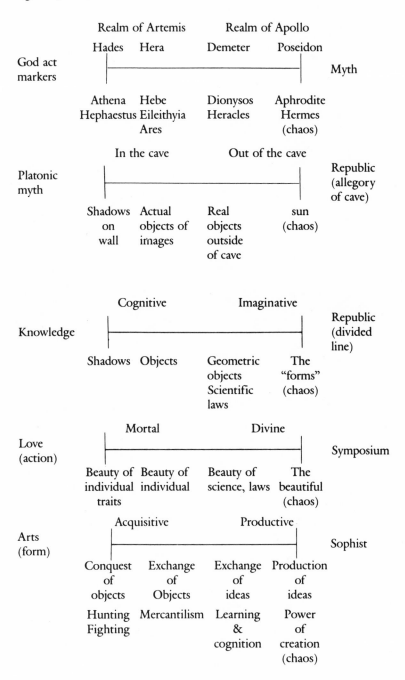

	Realm of Artemis	Realm of Apollo	
	Hades Hera	Demeter Poseidon	
God act markers			Myth
	Athena Hebe Hephaestus Eileithyia Ares	Dionysos Aphrodite Heracles Hermes (chaos)	

	In the cave	Out of the cave	
Platonic myth			Republic (allegory of cave)
	Shadows Actual on objects of wall images	Real sun objects (chaos) outside of cave	

	Cognitive	Imaginative	
Knowledge			Republic (divided line)
	Shadows Objects	Geometric The objects "forms" Scientific (chaos) laws	

	Mortal	Divine	
Love (action)			Symposium
	Beauty of Beauty of individual individual traits	Beauty of The science, laws beautiful (chaos)	

	Acquisitive	Productive	
Arts (form)			Sophist
	Conquest Exchange of of objects Objects	Exchange Production of of ideas ideas	
	Hunting Mercantilism Fighting	Learning Power & of cognition creation (chaos)	

Notes ❦

Introduction

1. This quote, as well as the quote in the Conclusion, is taken from Friedrich Nietzsche, *The Birth of Tragedy*, trans. Kaufmann (Random House, 1967), sec. 23.

2. The seminal work on this subject is Antonio de Nicolas, *Meditations through the Rg Veda*.

3. See Ernest McClain, *The Myth of Invariance*.

4. Because Greek mythology has suffered the most at the hands of myth theorists, I have decided to use its myths as the primary examples for this book; however, wherever relevant I shall also examine myths from other cultures.

5. The most startling example of Plato's awareness of this shift is seen at the end of the *Phaedrus*, where the myth of Thoth is told.

Chapter One

1. For an interesting discussion of this belief, see Joseph Campbell, *Oriental Mythology* (Penguin, 1962), 9–13, where he contrasts the Oriental and Occidental views of this notion by comparing the Brihadaranyaka Upanisad with the Genesis myth of the fall.

2. Rg Veda 10.129, in de Nicolas, *Meditations through the Rg Veda*, 229. In subsequent citations, "RV" denotes the Rg Veda.

3. *Mahanirvanatantra*, trans. Sir John Woodroffe (Dover Publications, 1972), 47–50.

4. For an excellent analysis of the Zero factor in the history of ideas, see Robert Lawlor, *Sacred Geometry*, 16–23.

5. Ernest McClain, *The Pythagorean Plato*, 131, quoting de Nicolas. An extensive study of the origin and criteria of the philosophical activity of oral/aural culture, as traced through the Hindu text of the Rg Veda, can be found in de Nicolas, *Meditations through the Rq Veda*. See also, McClain, *The Myth of Invariance*, 2–8, for a complete historical overview of this "musical hypothesis."

6. We shall discuss in the body of this book *how* this model of creation by One is an oral model. For now, the point being made is that different systems of knowledge emerge based upon one's epistemological framework.

7. Lawlor, *Sacred Geometry*, 19.

8. For a detailed account of the reign of Akhenaten and his influence on Egyptian culture, see D. Redford, *Akenaten* (Princeton University Press, 1984). See especially chapter 8, on the reign of the sun-disc.

9. Ibid., 157–58. To explore the complete Egyptian cosmological myth cycles would require an entire volume, though it is fascinating that these seemingly divergent myths can gain contextual uniformity when the model of sound as epistemology is the criterion for comparison. (See chapter 2).

10. Ibid., 180.

11. Ibid., chap. 8 (137–53).

12. St. Augustine, *Confessions,* trans. Pusey (Chicago, 1948), sec. 12.

13. See Plato's elaborate discussion of the One (albeit Parmenides view) in *Parmenides.*

14. This is the essence of the trainings of the mystery schools, and of the Pythagorean school.

15. Aristotle's discussion of substance occurs in book 12 of the *Metaphysics,* though the entire argument hinges upon the following statement: "and so what has always, from earlier times to now been looked for, and what has always remained in difficulty, namely, what is being. . . . [I]t is nothing other than substance" (*Met.* 1028b 2).

16. Ibid., bk. 12. This is precisely the shift that Plato feared and that is elaborately explained (in mythic form) in the *Phaedrus* (sec. 274c–end).

17. See René Descartes, *First Discourse on Optics* and *Discourse on Method.*

18. See the section of the Appendix called "Membering and Dismembering" for explanation of this point.

19. The most lucid religious/philosophical system that systematizes this belief into a distinct body of practice is the Orphic school. For a well-documented account of the mythological and philosophical tenets of Orphism, and for a detailed analysis of all the myths of Orphism, see M. L. West, *The Orphic Poems.*

20. de Nicolas, A., *Powers of Imagining*, 31–45.

21. You will discover in reading this book that there is a strong correlation between worship of the gods of Greece and exercising of the body. Specifically, the proper veneration of these deities does not occur through methods of worship as understood today; rather, these gods were made flesh through the human effort of exercising their own human capacities, the perfection of which represented the act of the god.

22. De Nicolas, *Meditations through the Rg Veda*, 224.

23. Translated by de Nicolas.

24. Translated by de Nicolas.

25. See P. O. Morford and J. Lenardon, *Greek Mythology* (Longman, 1985), 82–99, for an overview of the position of the gods and their major attributes.

26. Translated by de Nicolas.

27. Translated by Colavito.

28. Translated by de Nicolas. Compare this myth with Plato's myth of the creation of humans in the *Timaeus* for an interesting parallel. See also the creation of humans in *Genesis*.

29. Translated by Colavito.

30. The myth of Atlantis is found in Plato's dialogues *Timaeus* and *Critias*.

31. Trans. Desmond Lee (Penguin, 1971).

32. McClain, *The Myth of Invariance*, 73.

33. Trans. Lee (Penguin, 1971).

34. The reader is strongly advised to see the works of A. de Nicolas and, following him, E. McClain for the verification of this.

35. The bibliography on this is too extensive to even consider here. The origin of the word *myth* (Gr. "that which is spoken") alone would substantiate this claim.

36. *Meditations through the Ṛg Veda.*

37. De Nicolas establishes the criteria for a musical epistemology in the following passage from *Meditations through the Ṛg Veda:*

> Tone is a sound of a certain fixed pitch. No later than the third millennium B.C., and probably more than a thousand years earlier, man discovered that the intervals between tones could be defined by the ratio of the length of pipes and strings which sounded them. It was the ear that made ratios invariant; by its vivid memory of the simpler intervals, the ear made the development of the science of pure relations possible within the theory of numbers, the tone field now being isomorphic with the numbers field. From this musicalized number theory, which we know as "ratio theory," but which the ancients simply called "music," man began his model building. The ratios of the first six integers defined the building blocks: the octave, 1:2; the fifth, 2:3; the fourth, 3:4; the major third, 4:5; and the minor third, 5:6. From these first six integers,

functioning as multiples and submultiples of any reference unit (1) of length or frequency, a numerical cosmology was developed. (56)

38. Ibid., chap. 4–7.

Chapter Two

1. A very unique account of creation myths that does not limit itself to myths but extends the discussion to encompass science, art, and even poetry in a beautifully well-written manner is D. MacLagan, *Creation Myths* (Thames and Hudson, 1977).

2. Cyclical time is discussed in Campbell, *Oriental Mythology*, 3–9, though he doesn't refer to it as such. In Campbell's view, cyclical time is marked by the myth of the eternal return. See Mircea Eliade's work of this title, for a detailed account of the full meaning of this. See also Eliade's, *The Sacred and the Profane* (Harvest, 1959), 68–113.

3. In the model of music, chaos represents the uncut string, the realm of potentiality, containing the possibility for all tones though no tone has been actualized (i.e., no one has cut the string to release a tone).

4. Cosmos, in the musical model, is represented as any cut in the string, which sets up a tonal matrix upon which to build a tuning system (world).

5. The comparative myths to be discussed in the following section are only a small sampling of the exhaustive amount of comparative myth themes that have been examined by mythogrophers. Joseph Campbell's *The Masks of God* series is perhaps the most extensive comparative study done to date. Others have taken one particular myth theme and traced it

cross-culturally. A text of this sort that immediately comes to mind is Joseph Fontenrose's *Python*. Our purpose is *not* to merely note the cross-cultural similarities among myths; rather, this study is really concerned with finding the *reason for this affinity. The thesis here is that these myths are similar because they are all grounded on the same epistemology of sound.*

6. In *Enuma Elish*, A. Heidel, *The Babylonian Genesis* (University of Chicago Press, 1963), 18.

7. In de Nicolas, *Meditations through the Rg Veda*, 229.

8. Translation by Maria M. Colavito.

9. In West, *Orphic Poems*, 55.

10. See note 2, Introduction.

11. Translated by de Nicolas.

12. Translated by de Nicolas.

13. In West, *Orphic Poems*, 180.

14. Translated by de Nicolas.

15. In de Nicolas, *Meditations through the Rg Veda*, 229.

16. Translated by de Nicolas.

17. In de Nicolas, *Meditations through the Rg Veda*, 195.

18. Hesiod, *Theogony*, trans. Hendricks (Quill, 1972), 12.

19. In de Nicolas, *Meditations through the Rg Veda*, 229.

20. Translated by de Nicolas.

21. Trans. Hendricks, p. 12.

22. Ibid., 16.

Chapter Three

1. Hesiod, *Theogony,* trans. Hendricks, 10.

2. To aid the reader in this section, I have decided to offer a partial bibliography of ancient sources so that one can read about the exploits of the various gods under discussion from the written accounts in the myths themselves. Of course, any bibliography on Zeus is too exhaustive to offer entirely; however, the following list offers enough information to get one started:

Homer, *Iliad*
Hesiod, *Theogony*
Plautus, *Amphitryon*
Ovid, *Metamorphoses*
Cratylus Plato, 395e sq; *Timaeus* 41a; *Republic* 2.378a, 3.390b sq., 2.378d; *Phaedrus* 255c; *Symposium* 180e; *Laws* 12.94 lb; *Gorgias* 523e sq; et al.

3. As we have stated, Hades appears very little in the myths. The following sources contain some of the god's activities:

Homeric Hymn to Demeter 2
Ovid, *Metamorphoses* 5.359–424
Hesiod, *Theogony,* 453–506, 850
Apollodorus, 1.1.5–1.2.1, 1.3.2, 1.5.1–3, 2.5.12
Homer, *Iliad,* 5.844–45, 9.568–70

Hyginus, *Fabulae,* 79, 146
Plato, *Republic* 10.612b

4. Like Zeus, Poseidon's appearance in myth is rather extensive; therefore, the following partial list is offered:

Plato, *Cratylus* 402d sq.; *Gorgias* 523a; *Critias* 113c sq.; *Hippias Minor* 370c
Homer, *Iliad*; *Odyssey*
Hesiod, *Theogony,* 278–81, 453–06, 732–33; *Catalogue of Women,* 7, 9, 10, 13, 72
Homeric Hymn to Poseidon 22
Apollodorus
Herodotus, 7.129
Apollonius Rhodius, 1.179–89, 4.566–71
Hyginus, *Fabulae,* 89, 140, 166, 169, 186, 187–88; *Poetica Astronomica,* 2.5, 2.17, 2.20, 2.22
Ovid, *Metamorphoses,* 4.531–42, 2.547–95, 4.790–803, 6.115–20, 8.848–54
Vergil, *Aeneid,* 1.124–56, 5.779–d826

5. See W. O'Flaherty, *Shiva, the Erotic Ascetic,* (Oxford, 1973).

6. Hestia's position among the gods is discussed in the following accounts:

Hesiod, *Theogony,* 453–506
Homeric Hymn to Aphrodite 5.21–32
Homeric Hymns to Hestia 24, 33
Vergil, *Georgics,* 1408
Pausanius, 5.14.4
Plato, *Cratylus* 401b; *Phaedrus* 247a; *Laws* 9.855e sq., 5.745b, 8.848d

7. Homer's *Iliad* contains perhaps the best picture of Hera. See also:

Hesiod, *Theogony,* 326–32, 453–506, 921–34
Apollodorus, 1.4.3, 1.6.2, 1.7.4, 1.8.2, 1.9.8, 1.9.16, 1.9.2.28, 2.1.3–4, 2.2.2, 2.4.8, 2.4.12, 2.5.9–10, 2.7.7, 3.4.3, 3.5.1, 3.5.8
Ovid, *Metamorphoses,* 1.601–746, 2.466–533, 3.255–338, 3.362–69, 4.416–562, 6.90–97, 7.517–613, 9.280–323, 14.829–51
Plato, *Cratylus* 404b sq.; *Timaeus* 40d sq.; *Republic* 2.378d, 3.390b sq., 2.378d, 2.381d; *Laws* 6.774b sq.; *Phaedrus* 253b

8. Demeter is best described in the *Homeric Hymn to Demeter 2.* Other references are made to her in the following:

Ovid, *Metamorphoses,* 5.341–571, 5.642–61, 6.118–19, 8.738–878, 9.42–423
Pausanius, 8.15.1–4, 8.25.27–7, 8.37.6, 8.42.1–13
Hesiod, *Theogony,* 453–506, 912–14, 969–74
Homer, *Odyssey,* 5.125–28
Apollonius Rhodius, 4.986–90
Hyginus, *Fabulae,* 83
Plato, *Cratylus* 404b sq.; *Laws* 6.782b

9. Athena is a main character in both the *Iliad* and the *Odyssey* of Homer. She is also described in the following:

Hesiod, *Theogony,* 886–900, 924–29; *Catalogues of Women,* 7, 10
Hyginus, *Fabulae,* 142, 165, 168
Ovid, *Metamorphoses,* 4.790–803, 6.1–145, 8.251–53
Plato, *Laws* 11.920e sq., 1.626d, 7.80b, 7.796b sq., 5.745b, 8.848d; *Republic* 2.378c sq.; *Timaeus* 21e, 23d sq.; *Critias* 110b

10. Aside from Homer's *Iliad,* which contains, among other things, the two versions of Hephaestus's fall from heaven, the god appears in the following works:

Hesiod, *Theogony,* 570–72, 927–29, 945–46
Aeschylus, *Prometheus Bound*
Apollonius Rhodius, 1.202–205, 1.850–860
Pausanius, 1.20.3, 2.31.3, 8.53.5
Plato, *Cratylus* 404b, 407c, 391e; *Republic* 3.390c, 2.378d, 3.389a; *Protagoras* 321d sq.; *Timaeus* 23e; *Symposium* 192d sq.; *Critias* 109c; *Laws* 11.920e

11. See note 10, this chapter, for references to this in Plato.

12. Although Prometheus is not an Olympian, his position in *this* chapter is as a deity associated by acts performed with the two Olympians, Athena and Hephaestus. One should read Aeschylus, *Prometheus Bound,* to see how the myth of Prometheus applies here.

13. Ares is a main character in Homer's *Iliad.* See also:

Hesiod, *Theogony,* 921–23, 934–37
Apollodorus, *Library,* 1.4.4, 1.7.7, 1.8.2, 1.9.16, 2.5.8–9, 3.4.1–2, 3.5.5, 3.9.2, 3.14.8
Ovid, *Metamorphoses,* 15.862–63
Plato, *Cratylus* 407c sq.; *Republic* 3.390c; *Symposium* 196d; *Laws* 8.833b, 11.920e; *Phaedrus* 252c

14. Hebe is personified in Homer's *Iliad* and *Odyssey;* in Ovid, *Metamorphoses* (9.397–401, 9.416–17); and in Euripides, *Children of Heracles* (847–58)

15. Eileithyia appears in Pausanius (1.18.5, 2.22.6, 6.20.2–6, 8.21.3, 9.27.2), in Hesiod's *Theogony* (921–23),

and in the *Homeric Hymn to Apollo* (3.97–116). She appears in the plural form, Eileithyiae, in Homer.

16. This is the Orphic account of the birth of Dionysos. See West, *The Orphic Hymns,* for a detailed mythic account of this version.

17. Euripides, *The Bacchae,* represents the god Dionysos in the most lucid capacity. He also figures prominently in the following:

Apollodorus, *Library,* bk 3
Ovid, *Metamorphoses,* 3.513–4.41, 3.259–315, 4.389–419, 5.329, 7.294–96, 8.176–82, 11.67–84, 11.89–145, 13.650–74
Hesiod, *Theogony,* 940–42, 947–49
Homeric Hymns to Dionysos 1, 26
Aristophanes, *Frogs*
Plato, *Cratylus* 406b sq.; *Laws* 2.653d sq., 8.844d, 3.700b; *Phaedrus* 265b; *Ion* 534a; *Symposium* 1773; *Gorgias* 472a

18. Heracles is such a popular character that a list of sources containing his actions would be voluminous. It is best to read Euripides, *Heracles;* Sophocles, *Women of Trachis;* and Apollodorus (4.9.1–4.39.4) for the easiest overview of this hero's life.

19. Aphrodite figures prominently in Homer's *Iliad* and *Odyssey,* and in the *Theogony* of Hesiod (188–206, 975, 986–91). She is also discussed at length in Plato's *Symposium.* For other references to Aphrodite, see:

Ovid, *Metamorphoses,* 4.169–92, 4.285–388, 4.531–38, 5.331, 10.639–707, 14.484–511
Apollodorus, 1.3.3, 1.4.4, 1.9.17, 3.4.2, 3.14–3–4
Hyginus, *Fabulae,* 14–15, 40, 58, 92, 94, 147–48, 185

20. Hermes appears in both the *Iliad* and the *Odyssey* of Homer, as well as in the following:

Ovid, *Metamorphoses,* 2.685–835, 8.618–724, 11.303–17
Homeric Hymn to Hermes 4
Apollodorus, 1.6.2–3, 2.1.3, 2.4.2–3, 3.2.1, 3.4.3, 3.10.2
Plato, *Cratylus* 407e sq.; *Protagoras* 322c; *Phaedrus* 263d; *Laws* 12.941a; *Timaeus* 38d

21. See Barbara Walker, *The Woman's Book of Myths and Secrets* (Harper and Row, 1983), 397.

22. Geoffrey Hodson, *The Concealed Wisdom in World Mythology* (Adkyar, 1983), xxi.

23. For a complete analysis of the meaning of the androgyne, see E. Zola, *The Androgyne* (Crossroads, 1981). The myth of Hermaphroditus appears in Ovid, *Metamorphoses,* 4.285–388.

24. The *Homeric Hymn to Apollo* 3 describes his birth and subsequent appropriation of Delphi. He appears in Homer's *Iliad* and *Odyssey,* and in the following:

Hesiod, *Theogony,* 91–94, 346–48
Apollodorus, 1.3.2–4, 1.4.1–2, 1.7.8–9, 1.9.15, 2.5.9, 2.6.2, 3.10.1–4, 3.12.4
Ovid, *Metamorphoses,* 1.438–567, 2.535–632, 11.303–45, 14.129–53, 10.162–219, 10.106–42, 6.204–66, 6.382–400, 11.153–71
Plato; the references are too numerous to cite.

25. Artemis appears in Homer's *Iliad* and in the following:

Euripides, *Hippolytus*

Ovid, *Metamorphoses,* 3.138–252, 2.401–530, 5.330, 6.204–
312, 8.271–83, 11.321–27, 12.27–38, 15.487–551
Hyginus, *Fabulae,* 9, 53, 98, 122, 150, 189, 200

Chapter Four

1. According to the musical model, chaos as the uncut
string contains the unity of the whole of creation in potentia;
one has only to break it open by dividing the string in order
to freeze into existence a particular tone.

2. This is the Rta of the Hindu model; the exercise of
embodied movement that occurs when the musician is the
string and the two flow in harmonious unison. This model of
the singer and the song *is not metaphoric:* it is the exact description of how the gods function within this model. Like the
song of the singer, inherent in the string but unmanifest until
played, the gods embody the human spirit, but only through
the exercise of creation do they manifest. The sage knows to
keep all the gods present by his own action, the exercise of
which manifests the gods.

3. There are eight deities in this realm, because this is
the realm of the eternal return, metamorphosis, Samsara.
Here the bodies, upon death, remain within the sublunar
sphere, and after their elements separate, they become re-
created in another form. Musically, the number eight reflects
this point exactly, hence eight gods here. See McClain, *Myth of
Invariance,* chapter 2, for this explanation and, conversely, for
the reason why seven gods rule the realm of being.

4. The Pythagoreans held that Hestia was the divine
fire that animated the universe. Musically, Hestia is the center
because she represents the source from which, as well as the
source to which, all the tones return. As the octave matrix of

the Olympian pantheon, Hestia is not only the center, but the whole.

5. This effect is called "musical reciprocity." See Mc-Clain, Myth of Invariance, 23 for a detailed chart of how this functions in the musical model. For our purposes, it is alleged because of its importance to the role of free will in the mythical model, as it is customarily believed that mankind is predestined according to the mythic model. This view is completely without merit. In fact, the entire function of Greek tragedy reveals that while man is *destined to act, how* he acts and with what as a goal is entirely up to him. This is the message of tragedy: to act without attachment to the fruits of action is the way out of determinism because it is the way out of self. Hamartia occurs when one acts with an "I" as the actor; hubris occurs when one attributes action to that "I," because this focusing stops the flow of action by emphasizing an illusory substance, the actor. This is the skin of attachment. Aristotle knew this. When he defined tragedy, he said: "Tragedy is essentially an imitation not of persons but of action and life" (*Poetics*, 6.16).

6. *Sophrosyne* is a Greek word that is virtually undefinable in English. It describes a state of being for which we have no word because this state cannot exist in a literal worldview. The closest definition of Sophrosyne for us might be something like, "each part fit in its proper order," though if one were to imagine this to be like pieces of a puzzle that are all in order, one would *not* be understanding Sophrosyne. It is more like, using a musical analogy, the embodiment of all the possibilities of all the songs within the singer, such that at the appropriate moment, the appropriate song could be re-created. Achieving this state is the goal of ancient Greek education. It is done through the exercising of all the acts of all the gods, so that the proper god can be called upon when needed. It is the

ability to choose, from among the possible, the best (para-phrasing Plato).

7. See the Appendix for a visible musical description of this.

8. In other words, Apollo is the mediator between the one who first created the song (Zeus) and all of the subsequent human re-creators of it. When we re-create, musically we are performing both the same and the different songs with each recitation. We are slaying the dragon over and over again, as Apollo did on the model of Zeus.

9. Apollo's harmonia (equilibrium) is the image of Hestia because, by allowing no tone to reign supreme, he allows the capacity for all tones to live (Hestia).

10. See de Nicolas, *Powers of Imagining,* chap. 2.

Chapter Five

1. This is a compilation of the criteria that Pythagoras used, based on the *Vitae*. See the complete texts for verification.

2. See note 1.

3. This belief is the foundation of Orphism. For how Orphism is related to the Pythagorean system, see West, *The Orphic Poems.*

4. Guthrie, in *A History of Greek Philosophy,* vol. 1, writes:

They said too that the whole universe is constructed according to a musical scale . . . because it is both

composed of number and organized numerically
and musically. For the distances between the bodies
revolving around the center are mathematically
proportionate ... the sound made by the slower
bodies in their movement is slower in pitch, and
that of the faster is higher; hence, these separate
notes, corresponding to the ratios of the distances,
make the resulting sound concordant (284).

See also, Plato, *Phaedo*.

    5. Iamblichus, *Life of Pythagoras*, 61–65.

    6. See A. E. Taylor, *Plato: The Man and His Works*
(Meridian, 1956).

    7. Plato, *Republic*, trans. S. Buchanan (Viking, 1960),
542–45.

    8. Ibid., 546–51.

    9. Plato's criticism of the poets occurs on several
grounds. In book 10 (600c sq.) he says they are merely imitators, that is, they act from the realm of Artemis:

all the poetic tribe, beginning with Homer, are imitators of images of excellence and of the other
things that they "create" and do not lay hold on
truth ... knowing nothing but how to imitate.

In book 2 (2.377 sq.) he chastises them for being bad models
for the education of youth, because they offer bad models of
the gods, fashioned out of mortal qualities. Conversely, the
proper stories about the gods would induce the youth in such
a manner as to shape their souls:

When anyone images badly in his speech the true
nature of gods and heroes, . . . he is to blame.

The stories on the accepted list will induce nurses
and mothers to tell the children and so shape their
souls by these stories far rather than their bodies by
their hands.

These arguments taken as a whole are pointing to the fact that
poets in Plato's time were perceived by him as not *knowing* the
gods, when they spoke, but merely *knowing about* the gods.
This is his criticism: that their function, which was to keep
alive the story of how to make gods, was no longer being performed. They seemed to have sold out to the imitators. If the
poets were unable to keep the story alive, then their function
was useless in the republic. Of course, the Myth of Er at the
end of the dialogue mirrors this point, as Er, the witness,
*comes back to tell the story of his own experiences, and so the story
was kept alive.* Plato here is setting this myth against Homer's
myth of Hector. For more on this, see J. Bremer, *On Plato's
Polity* (Houston: Institute of Philosophy, 1984).

10. If one were to outline the speech of Diotima in the
Symposium (206b–212a), one would see that the speech is in
fact the same model as the divided line. See Appendix for
verification.

11. The claim in note 10 also holds true of the *Sophist*
(235c sq.).

Bibliography

Angus, S. *The Mystery Religions*. New York: Dover, 1975.

Apuleius, Lucius. *The Transformations of Lucius*. Translated by Robert Graves. New York: Farrar, Straus and Giroux, 1979.

Burckhardt, Titus, *Alchemy*. Worcester, England: Element Books, 1986.

Burkert, Walter. *Lore and Science in Ancient Pythagoreanism*. Cambridge: Harvard Univ. Press, 1972.

——— . *Structure and History in Greek Mythology and Ritual*. Berkeley: Univ. of California Press, 1979.

——— . *Greek Religion*. Cambridge: Harvard Univ. Press, 1985.

——— . *Ancient Mystery Cults*. Cambridge: Harvard Univ. Press, 1987.

Campbell, Joseph, ed. *The Mysteries*. Princeton: Princeton Univ. Press, 1978.

————. *The Masks of God.* Vols. 1–4. New York: Penguin, 1982.

————. *The Mythic Image.* Princeton: Princeton Univ. Press, 1974.

Clagett, Marshall. *Greek Science in Antiquity.* New York: Collier, 1963,

Clarke, M. L. *The Roman Mind.* New York: Norton, 1968.

Colavito, Maria *The Pythagorean Intertext in Ovid's Metamorphoses.* Lewiston: The Edwin Mellen Press, 1989.

Cornford, Francis. *Plato's Cosmology: The Timaeus of Plato.* London: Routledge and Kegan Paul, 1966.

————. *From Religion to Philosophy.* New York: Harper and Row, 1957.

Crump, M. M. *The Epyllion from Theocritus to Ovid.* New York: Garland, 1978.

Cumont, Franz. *Afterlife in Roman Paganism.* New Haven: Yale Univ. Press, 1959.

————. *Oriental Religions in Roman Paganism.* New York: Dover, 1956.

de Lubicz, R. A. Schwaller. *Sacred Science.* Translated by C. Vanden-Broeck. New York: Inner Traditions, 1982.

————. *The Temple in Man.* Translated by R. Lawlor. Vt. Inner Traditions International, 1977.

de Nicolas, Antonio. *Meditations through the Rg Veda*. New York: Nicolas-Hays, 1976.

————. *Powers of Imagining*. Albany: State Univ. of New York Press, 1980.

————. *Habits of Mind*. New York: Paragon House, 1989.

de Rola, Stanislas Klossowski. *Alchemy: The Secret Art*. London: Thames and Hudson, 1973.

Dicks, D. R. *Early Greek Astronomy to Aristotle*. Ithaca, N.Y.: Cornell Univ. Press, 1985.

Dijksterhuis, E. J. *The Mechanization of the World Picture*. Princeton: Princeton Univ. Press, 1986.

Diogenes Laertius. *Vitae Pythagoras*. Translated by R. D. Hicks. Cambridge: Harvard Univ. Press, 1979.

DuRocher, Richard. *Milton and Ovid*. Ithaca, N.Y.: Cornell Univ. Press, 1985.

Ferguson, John. *The Religions of the Roman Empire*. Ithaca, N.Y.: Cornell Univ. Press, 1982.

Fontenrose, Joseph *Python*. Berkeley: Univ. of California Press, 1980.

Gilchrist, Cherry. *Alchemy, The Great Work*. Northhamptonshire, England: Aquarian Press, 1984.

Godwin, Joscelyn. *Mystery Religions in the Ancient World*. San Francisco: Harper and Row, 1981.

————. *Harmonies of Heaven and Earth*. Vt. Inner Traditions International, 1987.

Gorman, Peter. *Pythagoras: A Life* London: Routledge and Kegan Paul, 1979.

Gottschalk, H. B. *Heraclides of Pontus*. Oxford: Clarendon Press, 1980.

Guthrie, W. K. C. *A History of Greek Philosophy*. Vol. 1. Cambridge: 1962.

————. *The Greeks and Their Gods*. Boston: Beacon Press, 1967.

Hall, Manly P., ed. *The Secret Teachings of All Ages*. Los Angeles: Philosophical Research Society, 1975.

Hamilton, Edith, and Cairns, Huntington, eds. *Plato: The Collected Dialogues*. Princeton: Princeton Univ. Press, 1982.

Harrison, Jane Ellen. *Themis*. New York: University Books, 1966.

Heath, Thomas, *A History of Greek Mathematics*. New York: Dover, 1981.

Iamblichus, *The Life of Pythagoras*. Translated by Thomas Taylor. Vt. Inner Traditions, 1986.

Ions, Veronica. *The World's Mythology*. London: Hamlyn Press, 1974.

Kirk, G. S., and Raven, J. E. *The Presocratic Philosophers*. Cambridge: Cambridge Univ. Press, 1975.

Lawlor, Robert. *Sacred Geometry*. New York: Crossroads, 1982.

Levy, Ernst. *A Theory of Harmony*. Albany: State Univ. of New York Press, 1985.

Levy, Ernst, and Levarie, S. *Tone: A Study in Musical Acoustics*. Kent, Ohio: Kent State Univ. Press, 1980.

Lloyd, G. E. R. *Early Greek Science: Thales to Aristotle*. New York: Norton, 1970.

Long, H. S. *A Study of the Doctrine of Metempsychosis in Greece from Pythagoras to Plato*. Ph.D diss., Princeton Univ., 1948.

Maziarz, Edward, and Greenwood, Thomas, *Greek Mathematical Philosophy*. New York: Frederick Ungar, 1968.

McClain, Ernest. *The Myth of Invariance*. New York: Nicolas-Hays, 1976.

———. *The Pythagorean Plato*. New York: Nicolas-Hays, 1978.

Mookerjee, Ajit. *Kali: The Divine Feminine*. New York: Destiny Books, 1988.

Muller-Ortega, Paul. *The Triadic Heart of Siva*. Albany: State Univ. of New York Press, 1989.

Nahm, Milton, ed. *Selections from Early Greek Philosophy*. New York: Appleton, 1962.

d'Olivet, Fabre. *Vers Dores des Pythagoriciens*. New York: Putnam's, 1917.

O'Meara, Dominic, ed. *Neoplatonism and Christian Thought.* Albany: State Univ. of New York Press, 1982.

Otis, Brooks. *Ovid as an Epic Poet.* Cambridge: Cambridge Univ. Press, 1966.

Ovid. *Metamorphoses.* Translated by Mary Innes. Baltimore: Penguin Books, 1955.

Philip, J. A. *Pythagoras and Ancient Pythagoreanism.* Toronto: Toronto Univ. Press, 1966.

Philostratus. *Life of Apollonius.* Translated by C. P. Jones. Baltimore: Penguin Books, 1970.

Raven, J. E. *Pythagoreans and Eleatics.* Cambridge: Cambridge Univ. Press, 1948.

Rose, H. J. *Religion in Greece and Rome.* New York: Harper and Row, 1959.

Sargent, Thelma, ed. *The Homeric Hymns.* New York: Norton, 1975.

Saunders, Jason, ed. *Greek and Roman Philosophy after Aristotle.* New York: Free Press, 1966.

Scott, Walter, Trans. and ed. *Hermetica.* Boston: Shambhala, 1985.

Sebeok, Thomas, ed. *Myth a Symposium.* Bloomington: Indiana Univ. Press, 1965.

Tejera, Victorino. *Modes of Greek Thought.* New York: Appleton, 1971.

———. *Plato's Dialogues One by One.* New York: Irvington, 1984.

Timaios of Locri. *On the Nature of the World and the Soul.* Translated by Thomas Tobin. Chicago: Scholars Press, 1985.

Vanderbroeck, Andre. *Philosophical Geometry.* Vt. Inner Traditions International, 1987.

Vogel, C. J. *Pythagoras and Early Pythagoreanism.* Van Gorcum, 1961.

West, M. L. *The Orphic Poems.* Oxford: Clarendon Press, 1984.

Wheelwright, Philip, ed. *The Presocratics.* Indianapolis: Bobbs-Merrill, 1985.

Wilbur, J. B., and Allen, H. J. *The Worlds of the Early Greek Philosophers.* New York: Prometheus Books, 1979.

Wilkinson, L. P. *Ovid Recalled.* Cambridge: Cambridge Univ. Press, 1955.

Wright, M. R. *Empedocles: The Extant of Greek Fragments.* New Haven: Yale Univ. Press, 1981.

Zeller, Eduard. *Outlines of the History of Greek Philosophy.* New York: Meridian, 1969.

Index 🌿

DATE DUE

HIGHSMITH 45-220

THE NEW THEO...
MYTHOLOGY FOR THE ...

Maria M. Colavito

This book is a sustained focus on those original human acts that gave us the gods, the human psyche, and the stories about them. Dr. Colavito divides myth into four distinct but inseparable "acts": first is the original power to create; second, the stories about the manifestation; third, the imitation and duplication of the manifested images; and fourth, the theories regarding the first three. Development of these four "acts" provides the foundation for studying and interpreting myth cross–culturally.

"What I like most about this book are the possibilities it suggests. Maria Colavito's ideas constitute a new hermeneutical approach to the Greek myths that pushes the reader to consider (or reconsider) the relevancy of these myths, their potential function as meaningful paradigms for the reader's life. The ideas outlined by the author are inherently important. At the same time, they will prove to be a valuable contribution to the study of western esotericism, an increasingly important area which is being carved out by scholars like Ioan P. Couliano and Antoine Faivre. The author's bold insistence on a connection between the meaning of myth and the embodied praxis of certain followers of Plato and Pythagoras is far-reaching in its implications. This book has the potential to transform, rather than merely inform, its readers."

—Karen Voss, San Jose State University

Maria M. Colavito teaches Mythology at the University of North Florida and is the President of the Mythic Arts Institute of America. She is the author of *The Pythagorean Intertext in Ovid's Metamorphoses.*

STATE UNIVERSITY OF NEW YORK PRESS

ISBN 0-7914-1068-4

90000>

9 780791 410684